Reels, Rock and Rosaries

Confessions of a Newfoundland Musician

Marjorie Doyle

Pottersfield Press, Lawrencetown Beach, Nova Scotia, Canada

Copyright © 2005 Marjorie Doyle

All rigthts reserved. No part of this publication may be reproduced or used or transmitted in any form or by any means – graphic, electronic or mechanical, including photocopying – or by any information storage or retrieval system, without the prior written permission of the publisher. Any requests for photocopying, recording, taping or information storage and retrieval systems of any part of this book shall be directed in writing to Access Copyright, The Canadian Copyright Licensing Agency, 1 Yonge Street, Suite 1900, Toronto, Ontario M5E 1E5 (www.accesscopyright.ca). This also applies to classroom use.

Library and Archives Canada Cataloguing in Publication

Doyle, Marjorie M.,
Reels, rock and rosaries : confessions of a Newfoundland musician / Marjorie Doyle.

ISBN 1-895900-73-5

1. Doyle, Marjorie M., - 2. Broadcasters--Canada--Biography.
3. Journalists--Newfoundland--Biography. 4. Musicians--Canada--Biography.
5. Music--Newfoundland--Anecdotes.

PN1990 .72.D75A3 2005   384.54'092   C2005-902639-1

Cover design: Dalhousie Design Services

Pottersfield Press acknowledges the ongoing support of The Canada Council for the Arts, and the financial support of the Government of Canada through the Book Publishing Industry Development Program for our publishing actuivities. We also acknowledge the support of the Nova Scotia Department of Tourism, Culture and Heritage.

Pottersfield Press
83 Leslie Road
East Lawrencetown
Nova Scotia, Canada, B2Z 1P8
Website: www.pottersfieldpress.com
To order, phone 1-800-NIMBUS9 (1-800-646-2879)
Printed in Canada

 Canada Council   Conseil des Arts   Canadä
for the Arts   du Canada

Contents

Introduction	5
Those Sly Tunes	12
The Mute Harp	18
My Uncles Didn't Dance	32
The March of My Soul	49
On Poplar Avenue	55
The Practice Room	66
The Walrus and the Nun	73
The Holiness Crowd	89
Mr. Foggin's Fellows Come to Town	99
Patsy, Dolly, Gustav, Franz	112
Dinner Music	120
The Disappearing Concert	129
A Chorus Girl Away	140
A Chorus Girl at Home: Sing, and Louder Sing	148
Conclusion	156
Acknowledgements	159

About the Author

Marjorie Doyle was born in St. John's, Newfoundland. She received an M.A. from Memorial University in 1987. For ten years she worked as a broadcaster on various CBC radio shows, including five years as host of *That Time of the Night*. She was a columnsit with *The Globe and Mail*, a music columnist with the St. John's *Evening Telegram*. She's published in the *Ottawa Citizen*, *This Magazine*, and the *Dictionary of Canadian Biography*.

Also by Marjorie Doyle

A View of Her Own
Newfoundlander in Exile: The Life and Times of Philip Tocque 1814-1899

Versions of some of these pieces have appeared in magazines

"The Mute Harp" in *The Fiddlehead* No. 23, Spring 2005.

"My Uncles Didn't Dance" (winner of the Silver Award, Essay Category, National Magazine Awards, 2005) in *Queen's Quarterly* Vol. 111, No. 2, Summer 2004.

"The March of My Soul (as "My Public Private Parts") in *Newfoundland Quarterly* Vol. 96, No. 2, Summer 2003.

An excerpt from "The Walrus and the Nun" (as "Goin' to MUN") in *Geist* No. 55, 2005.

"Mr. Foggin's Fellows Come to Town" in *The Antigonish Review* No. 141/142, 2005.

"Dinner Music" won a 2003 Newfoundland and Labrador Arts and Letters Award for non-fiction prose.

"Sing and Louder Sing" and "The Practice Room" (as "Wandering Thoughts and Solitary Hours") were both short-listed for the 2004 Larry Turner Award.

Introduction

I remember my first book.

    The cover is light green, uncluttered; the title and scant information, mysterious to me at the time, appears in a darker green. In the centre of this pale sea floats a small, stark image – a silhouette of the island of Newfoundland; floats but surely is anchored because it is fixed and solid.

    The island's configuration is rich, intricately designed as if the geo-gods of rock and glacier made merry mapping us out – grinding out inlets and coves by the thousands around six thousand miles of rocky coastline. Is that how we came to be? Or did celestial artisans work the land like putty, molding and shaping, pushing and pulling? Or perhaps child gods drawing on a sandy beach grabbed a shared stick from one another saying: I want to shove this in, poke that out. However it happened, we've ended up on a distinctive rock. Who, having seen the map of the island of Newfoundland, cannot identify it again?

    Perhaps that is why the small green book – not a myopic view of my thumb, not the bottle (I mean the baby bottle) – is my primal image, the first one I remember, the one that has endured. That wanna-be triangle with its long deep bays and small jagged coves sent its curious peninsulas out to me. They crawled into my mus-

Silhouette of the island of Newfoundland, my first remembered image

cles, bones, and sinews carrying a message: Newfoundland was an island country, and we a people.

The facts belie this. By the time I was born, Newfoundland had become a province of Canada, but I cannot say for sure when that news reached me – maybe a couple of years ago at a cocktail party? But that we were a nation apart, that there was an "us" wrapped up in that tiny figure was clear to me. The cover told a story: the vastness and expanse of the implied water declared a gulf between us and others. And, as in the tongue-in-cheek maps of the world sold here as souvenirs, the location of the island proclaimed Newfoundland as the centre of the world.

Was this, the cover design of my father's 1955 *Old-Time Songs of Newfoundland*, his ultimate act of patriotism?

The silhouette, a lone raft in a clear sea, sat temptingly on the cover, as alluring as a desktop icon. I double clicked at an early age, and walked in. Walked into pages of sailors and loggers, sealers and lovers, roaming the waters and beaches of some certain country. I couldn't read, but others could and when they gathered around the piano at home to sing, I held up my book, turned pages and jumped in when I could grab onto a familiar word or line. It was like skipping Double Dutch with bigger kids – the grown-ups were efficient, faster and I could only hope to dodge in when something familiar whizzed by. I rhymed off the names of "Jim Fling, Tom Ring and Johnson, champion of the ring" piling into a soiree at Kelligrews, a party already jam-packed with "Jim Brine, Din Ryan, Flipper Smith and Caroline." I sang about the O'Hooligans hosting a tea party with a cake so tough that "two sealers attacked it with hand-spikes to try to remove the top crust." There was Jim Long boasting about how to get the girl you want, the braggart Jack Hinks, rebels, pranksters, and sooks whining about unrequited love.

Balladeers, some long gone, most with their identities forgotten, had eavesdropped, spied, recorded incidents they'd witnessed and stories they'd heard. Sometimes faithful photographers, sometimes imaginative painters, they left us with the details and drama of lives lived on and around a cold sea. I didn't always understand the lyrics of our songwriters who, far from the shores of the American dream, recorded also that hard work leads to more hard work, and often to a cycle of futility and bitterness.

> Two dollars they'll pay you for piling up timber,
> And then eighteen dollars for board they will take,
> And then they will take six dollars for blankets;
> And that's how you're soaked on the shores of Twin Lakes.
>
> ("Twin Lakes")

It was bustling in those pages: competitive whalers racing across the Atlantic; men (real men, names listed) fighting storms at sea, sometimes winning, often not. Stories of seals caught, lives lost, a litany of shipwrecks, and tales of high jinks on the squid-jigging ground. The songs described not the beauty of the land, but the power of the sea. It was an aural jumble to a small child, but breathless and vivid. After a night of singing the songs from my little green book, I fell into bed exhausted from travels around my vibrant island country.

This was my earliest music. Then, a few years later, I rose from a small oak desk in my grade one classroom, and took my first steps into that expansive country of classical music. The entryway was my first piano lesson.

It was momentous: the departure from the safe, known world of school across no man's land to the adjoining convent, tentatively creeping along the wide dark corridor lit only by a red vigil lamp, arriving at last into a bright open palatial room, Mother Patricia's parlour. The aged nun, the height of the ornate ceilings, the grandeur of the windows flashed that this was a life-changing moment. In the coming weeks, as the curious blotches on the page unscrambled and connected with the black and white piano keys, the miracle of reading music was mine. How was I so lucky – why me, to have this grand introduction, to decipher a foreign language that would ease me into a lifetime of riches and plenty, the gift given early, the gift no child should be deprived of. And where that led! To glee club, where I swear I levitated when I first heard four-part harmony, where I myself was in the bundle of notes creating that marvel of sound, in the crush, the warm squeeze, the dissonance waiting to resolve. The simple skill of musical literacy led to friendships, to travel, to a passport that permitted entry to musical ensembles anywhere. Led to a place where street language doesn't matter, where a greater shared language transcends all. Led to a key to a private club that has branches all over the world.

Then orchestral music gathered me up and lured me into a sea of chords and colours, of harmonies parading by, of melodies chasing one another. It offered the wild ride through Leonard Bernstein's overture to *Candide*; I, the piccolo player, surfing above the orchestra then falling, falling into a hole dug by panic and terror, the hole where the solo's supposed to be. And next night getting a second crack at it, certain I'll make it this time, and yes I arrive, right at the spot where the solo comes, no hole this time – just a small crash landing on the wrong note.

Classical music stood fast, but Newfoundland music swirled around me, too. In the 1970s a ground swell of nationalism pushed traditional music forward, energizing and recreating it, and I embraced all that – getting a phone call from an excited friend with hot news: The Duff (Figgy Duff) would be playing here, or singing there – saying yes, yes to all of it, and all of it gloriously tied to a new heightened expression of patriotism, revelling in the swelling numbers of those who felt the passion, grabbed music as a vehicle, grasped it as a symbol.

This was in my early working years; I tagged along with the crowd, taking on the habits of reporters from the old days, coursing late night watering holes. Released from our Duckworth Street newsroom, we would escape into the circuit of The Cochrane, The Welcome, Freddy's (The Royalton), Bridgett's, The Belmont, Dirty

Dick's – ending up in after-hours hideaways at 4:00 a.m., worn out from dancing jigs and reels with fallen and falling colleagues. Our heels and toes cast about in those fly away gestures – joy, pride and anger all kicked up in those flying steps. Never-ending energy pushing never-ending music. You couldn't stop, even though your sore, aching hips begged you to. If you dropped down dead, they'd dance around you, because who could rein in the pulsing rhythm, who could abandon the dance?

I could. One foot was lodged there in the traditional music revival but, no matter how grand it was, no matter how true, my other foot itched to head home to lose myself in recordings of Elly Ameling singing Schubert or Georg Solti conducting Brahms. I listened to traditional music with one ear, just waiting to trot off next night to orchestra practice, flute tucked protectively under my arm, squirming a little knowing that for some, in those days, the house of Newfoundland nationalism held no room for classical music.

The flute, too, got tangled up in the opposing impulses of my musical life. I canvassed the town until I found a jeweller brave enough and skilled enough to drill a hole into my precious silver Haines flute. He soldered on a tiny metal plate so I could snap on a microphone. On Tuesdays and Sundays I would attend orchestra rehearsals for a Haydn Symphony or a Tchaikovsky piano concerto; the rest of the week I pretended I was Jethro Tull or Herbie Mann. The waves of rock music tossed me into a hazy new world of enhanced listening, lost in the roar of the Rolling Stones and Pink Floyd. Rock hung around – I grabbed it, rolled in it when I needed to convince myself I'd travelled beyond the long arm of the convent school. But when I sought ecstasy, exhilaration or catharsis, I hauled out recordings of Schumann and Brahms and let their great symphonies wash over me. I was always in the closet, bumping around contradictions, even today in aerobics class where I can bounce and flop and bop to music I am officially in rebellion against. (I disguise myself to maintain a healthy public disassociation from pop, disco and other low-lying musical disorders.) Country music came late. No coincidence that just as I needed the hurtin' songs, the hurtin' songs arrived – I simply hadn't "heard" them before. When Patsy Cline strutted in with her raw, earthy sensibility, the pining heroes of Franz Schubert were shoved out – but only temporarily.

Music kept circling me. Wherever I moved, music was there too. I fell into broadcasting and after commentary, journalism and satire, I settled comfortably into hosting *That Time of the Night* on CBC Radio, a late-night classical music program. The intimacy of radio and the vulnerability that steals in at night brought stacks of letters from restless insomniacs, solitary night-shift workers and vigil-keepers watching over the ill and the dying. Truck drivers on their long-distance runs kept company with the show, as did young lovers like Lindsay M. in Edmonton and Mark S. in Regina. They were in a long-distance relationship. They lay in separate beds, in distant cities, linked by music they were listening to "together."

The power of music was not news to me. Not since sitting in a box in an opera house, Gran Teatre del Liceu in Barcelona, close enough to sweat and tremble with Agnes Baltsa and José Carreras as they lured us into the passion and horror of Georges Bizet's *Carmen*. No, the power of music was not new to me – not since I'd had to forsake choral music in the early years of my apostasy, because the childhood knot of music and religion was too tight to undo. The daily mail to the radio show brought not news, but a reminder that notes and chords are loaded with pleasure and pain, that for many the trigger for memory, more than taste or smell or even photographs, is aural. A reminder that the stream that flows between now and then, between present and past, is music.

In Newfoundland music, the themes have changed since the songs of my childhood. Many songwriters now are the voice of the migrant worker; themes are often home, emigration, yearning and longing. Those away are nostalgic for home, those here nostalgic for the past. Around the letters, profiles, memories and photos in the glossy magazine *The Downhomer*, the Newfoundland saga unfolds in the pages of advertisements for moving companies and real estate. In all the shifting and resettling, the coming and going, music stands as connector.

A few years ago my eighty-eight-year-old aunt travelled from Arizona to St. John's to attend her sister's (my mother's) birthday. She'd left Newfoundland in the 1940s and had been back maybe two or three times. There was music in our houses each evening she was here – either us playing and singing around the piano, or recordings in the background. On one of those nights, she was relating to me a story about the distant past when suddenly she stopped speaking, drifted off. She was listening. The Walsh family CD *The Passing of the Years* was playing. My aunt turned to me and said, "The only time I hear music is when I'm home." Home. She'd been gone sixty years. It's not possible that she hadn't heard music in a lifetime of raising children and grandchildren, but what she'd heard passed her by until that moment, when a clear, sweet voice sang a sentimental song that wound its way deep into the soul of this Newfoundland emigré.

The shape of the island of Newfoundland has been forged into brooches and pendants, and it hangs as earrings off the heads of young and old. It's imprinted on jackets, t-shirts, scarves, and lingerie. (And yes, there are tattoos.) Are we peculiar? Are the inhabitants of Alberta and Ontario roaming the world with little Canadas dangling off their necks? That first image of mine, that small odd triangle poked and prodded with permutations and indentations, is for me more than a geological formation. It is a symbol of place, home, nationhood.

It is against these two backdrops of Newfoundland and music that my life has fallen.

Those Sly Tunes

Music can deafen you. It can scream so loudly your surroundings disappear and you are left with a small song inside. It can come like a gale force wind, and batter you a little. Or like a twister: the notes gather you up, you lose your footing, your breath. Sometimes it's like that, music. Or maybe it swans into your territory, like the hint of lilac in early summer, a tender greeting first. Then its fragrance grows stronger and streams inside you and unleashes another year, and another, back to memories of the first lilac time. Music: loaded notes and melodies tramping alongside you, up and down cemetery rows, or taking you on a pub crawl through alleys of forgotten loves; walking you through pleasant fields or dropping you hard in a cold puddle.

I rented an apartment once in a small town in the American midwest. All the apartments in the building had outside entrances so there was no mixing with other tenants. I saw the guy next door maybe once or twice. My first night there, I heard a song coming from his apartment. I didn't recognize the singer and couldn't actually hear the words. Had there been a crime committed in that apartment and I'd been called before a forensic musicologist, the most I could have offered was that it was a pop song. When I left the flat six months later, I still didn't know the particulars, but the tune had worked itself inside me, insinuating itself as the song crept again and again through the walls. It had been a slow progression, beginning with "Damn! If he only likes one song why can't it be Mahler?" But in time, it offered familiarity, and a kind of consolation. It meant buddy was home, took some of the lonesomeness out of apartment living, and created the illusion that I had a connection with the guy next door. It never did pique my curiosity enough to seek out the name of the song and after I moved away, I forgot about it.

Some time later I had a Rigoletto-style moment – you know, Rigoletto, believing he is holding in his arms the body of the Duke whom he's paid to have killed, hears the Duke singing his signature song in the distance. OK, it's not *exactly* the same, but a year or two after my time in that tiny apartment in Lemoine Village, I was in a cab and there it was on the radio, the song from next door. And now the DJ unravelled the mystery: Billy Joel (Billy who?) singing "She's Always a Woman To Me." My neighbour had lived alone and didn't seem to have a girlfriend but there must have been a time when it was "their song"; then it became "his" song after she left. (Dumped him? Died?) Now it was "our song" – mine and his, that is – except of course he didn't know about the transference.

I don't seek out this song, but from time to time, it turns up and when it does, as soon as I hear a note of it, I am back in Lemoine Village in that squatty grad-school kitchen. I can taste the soybean stew and the corn chowder I lived on at the time. During that same year I was singing in a choir that performed magnificent choral works and I played catchy Duke Ellington tunes in a stage band, but the music that carries the memories and can dump me back there in an instant is that one undistinguished pop song, only ever heard through those paper walls. As with the eavesdropper on Wordsworth's solitary reaper, the "music in my heart I bore, long after it was heard no more."

Music does that – a few notes here, a phrase there and off you float from the here-and-now to the back-then. Think of last waltzes from high school. Whenever I hear Simon and Garfunkel's "Bridge Over Troubled Water," my hand flies to my mouth in a desperate protective gesture to ward off, retroactively, that shocking first kiss. And certainly with every semiquaver of Latin I sing, I am immediately lifted from my present and flung back to my grammar school glee club. The holiness faucet is turned on and this atheist (maybe agnostic, perhaps just heretic) recedes and faith and hope (plus charity on a good day) rekindle and flow.

I keep a song list, an emotional hit parade, ready for the day my courage leads me to the therapist's door. I will walk in with a Discman and a handful of CDs. Let's start with the Mozart, doc, I'll say, then the Billy Joel, followed by "Hey Jude," the Brahms *Alto Rhapsody* . . . And slowly I'll work my way through the loaded notes to Wordsworth's "natural sorrow, loss or pain that has been and may be again."

Once when I was getting married, the groom and I met with the DJ to discuss music for the reception. We talked about the first dance, parents' dance, last dance, and then the DJ said, "What about your 'do nots'?"

"Your due-knots?"

"Your do-nots. Your 'do not play this song under any circumstances.' There must be some."

Ah yes, those. The list, and it can be a long one, of all the songs that are going to trigger pain, misery, or jealousy for one or both of the pair. I laughed first, but sobered up quickly enough. There's . . . I sure wouldn't want to hear *that* in the middle of my wedding celebration. And then there's . . ., definitely to be avoided. The more times you have been up the aisle, the more pieces you have to remember to forbid. You might be walking down the same road to doom but at least on that first day, you want to travel light – no baggage. I met a woman once who told me there were forty-two songs on her Do Not list. She auditioned three DJs before she could find one with enough songs he could play with impunity.

I moved to Spain in the late eighties. I took two suitcases. At first, the stay was to be for one year, and even when it spilled over into a second, I acquired very little. It was in that long ago era of cumbersome vinyl recordings; records didn't travel well, as CDs do, and we had no stereo. What I did have was a Sony Walkman, which I used to learn Spanish by listening to the radio, and three cassettes – the soundtrack of *Amadeus*, *The Magic Flute*, and Schubert's *Symphony No. 9*. Working in Barcelona was exhausting and when the weekends came I couldn't face the crowds, the metro, the buses, the requisite maze to get to a record store.

The only shopping I did was in my neighbourhood in the fruteria, the patisserie, the charcuterie and most importantly the bodega, where generous amounts of good wine were available, cheap. No fooling around here with fancy labels and corks – just bring in the old empty and fill 'er up, much like years ago taking a gallon bottle to a gas station for fuel for an outboard motor. My shopping district and priorities so defined, I never did manage to procure more cassettes.

Every day when I rode my stationary bicycle (that *was* a crazy time of my life: *I worked out!*), I listened to *The Magic Flute*. That period of my life was bittersweet and even now, more than fifteen years later, when I hear the section where the Three Boys sing outside the temple, I gasp, partly from the exquisite boys' voices blended so perfectly in a harmonically simple, melodically beautiful trio. There is an innocence, a purity, a gentleness. It is as if the music comes out of these boys as nonchalantly as "Hi, how are you," with the singers unaware of the transcendence they bring about in a listener. I wince, too, because it triggers so vividly my time in Barcelona. I had arrived as part of a twosome; I left alone.

A piece of music will do that; it will unleash memory so dramatically that Proust's madeleine is reduced, by comparison, to a dried up raisin square. (When the French writer Marcel Proust dunked a pastry into his tea one day, the taste unexpectedly unlocked the childhood memories that produced his voluminous *Remembrance of Things Past*). Hints of a line from an earlier time, snatches of forgotten melodies, they're scattered all around like land mines and one innocent step – in a restaurant, in someone's living room, in a cab with the radio on – can cause an explosion. Even the workplace.

I hosted a radio show, *That Time of the Night*, for some years; it was a gratifying way to earn a living, spending the day listening to pieces of music, thinking about them, talking about them, and then listening again, with company. Every morning I would stick on a headset and listen to CDs to program for the show, a late-night classical music program. The headset had a long cord which allowed me a degree of physical movement: while I was listening,

I could open the window, sharpen my pencil, walk to our reference shelf and take down a book. One day I was at the end of my rope, so to speak, trying to reach something in a filing cabinet several feet away as I was auditioning a new CD of piano music. Suddenly I froze. And in an instant I was out of that radio station on Duckworth Street in St. John's and in the nursery of my childhood home. Unwittingly, I'd taken another bite out of that aural madeleine. I had not even remembered there'd been a music box in my room, a music box which had played one piece: the second theme of Chopin's *Fantaisie Impromptu*. Now I could see it vividly, a green marble music box in the shape of a grand piano; when you opened the lid, the piano played.

But if I was sitting in the studio having tumultuous moments, so were listeners at home in bed, working nightshifts, nursing their sick, commuting, and travelling on long-distance drives. They wrote me – warm letters, funny letters, thoughtful letters. The most heart-stopping described private moments when a piece of music yanked a listener from the present to some loaded, perhaps forgotten, past. Sometimes the letters told of a dying friend or relative finding comfort in a particular piece of music. Sometimes they told of the joy of recovering a lost memory. Always, listeners were moved.

In the Motherhouse of the Presentation Sisters in St. John's, there is a small marble sculpture of the head of the Virgin, created by the nineteenth-century Italian sculptor Giovanni Strazzo. It's called The Veiled Virgin. Her face is finely chiselled. Draped over her face is a transparent veil, also chiselled out of marble. Its folds fall over the detailed visage with its perfectly executed eyes, nose, lips; her eyelashes are visible. The Sisters are generous about visiting. When I go, I draw in my breath at the sheer beauty. I can scarcely believe the veil is part of the sculpture, that it is not a delicate covering tenderly placed over the statue by protective nuns, but no: this is a work of genius. My response is awe.

There's a deeper layer in music, beyond appreciation of craft and art, and not related to theme or story. Music is organized sound with a mysterious power to reach our deepest spots. A piece of music can make us halt our actions; we dare not stir or pursue other activities until the last note dies away. Listen to the slow movement of Schubert's *Quintet in C* – it is as if the strings are weeping together. Or listen to the adagietto for strings and harp from Gustav Mahler's *Symphony No. 5*. There is grief here, but it is greater than any personal or private grief; this is an extended exploration of universal despair. The violins, violas, cellos pass the melody back and forth as if no one section can bear the music. They must share the angst or they will collapse under its weight. When the cellos come to the end of a phrase, sounding as if they will deplete emotionally any moment, the violins pick up and finish for them. Throughout, the solemn harp wanders, tolling, suggestive. The fragile must turn away from this piece. Or listen to it in preparation for a visit with a therapist, or a retreat to some refuge where one can go and sort out the sore spots.

Poetry can move me. W.H. Auden's lament "Stop all the clocks/ cut off the telephone . . . " (IX from *Twelve Songs*) expresses the fullness of love and then grief at the loss of one's lover. A passage from a novel, a gripping soliloquy in theatre – they can find my raw centre, but not as music can. Music is more potent, more immediate, more accessible. And it is ubiquitous – in shops, offices, bars, cars, at weddings and funerals and any formal ceremonies, there is music. Most people are more likely to hear a piece of music on any given day than to hear a poem, or see a play. We seek out the other arts; music hangs around. We had best be wary: in a few notes our hearts may betray us, their well-shored walls crumbling, leaving us to face the music and what it carries.

I tread carefully now, picking my way through life as if it's Hallowe'en and I'm a child crossing a lawn where a playful homeowner has planted ghosts to scare the little kids. Slowly I let my peripheral vision admit the partly outlined spook on the right, the scary triangle of the witch's hat on the left and bang! I hightail it to the sidewalk – who wants that sour apple anyway? It's like that, except it's not Hallowe'en, it's every day and I'm a grown-up, and the spooks and owls are quarter notes and blues riffs and snatches of a string quartet. I take cautious steps, gingerly testing the ground, knowing they are out there, those sly tunes, weighted with memory, circling me, ready to sneak up and pounce.

The Mute Harp

I've heard my brothers say that in the old days, before I was born, there was a ritual in our house on March 17. The first boy (there were seven) to get up in the morning, rush to Dad and sing, "Get up ye devil and play the fiddle, St. Patrick's Day is daaawwwwwning," would collect a nickel or a quarter. My father died before I was old enough to sing an Irish ditty – or anything else – but St. Patrick's Day was still kept. On our flagpole we raised an Irish flag, a gold harp on a green background, and we broke our Lenten fast with glee, eating all the chocolates we could stuff in during the one day reprieve. The weather was probably wintry, but my memory has preserved it as spring-like, probably clinging to one warm St. Patrick's Day. It's relative: in the midst of Newfoundland's "lean and hungry month of March," St. Patrick's Day in some years possibly did bring that first whiff of warmth in the wind, and the sight of stiff straw-like grass and frozen earth. It was a holiday, breathing onto the town that idle comfort of timelessness, lost forever since Sunday shopping arrived. We would go to Mass as a family, grateful to see drab winter brightened with colourful banners and flags streaming from the Basilica of St. John the Baptist and from the Benevolent Irish Society (B.I.S.) across the street. At home, there were visitors. At night we sang around the piano from thick Irish songbooks: contemporary collections published in America and a red hardcover book from ancient Ireland – Dublin 1882, to be exact

– of *Moore's Irish Melodies*. Latter-day inventions such as the sobriquet "Paddy's Day" and dyeing your beer green – I suppose it's your hair now – were not part of it, although we did wear shamrock brooches and pins. Given that I've never had a similar Ukrainian or Chinese experience, and my family has never marked Polish feasts or Robbie Burns day, you might think me Irish.

On both my parents' sides of the family, the heritage is Irish, Irish, and then some. But am *I* Irish? My foremothers and forefathers have been in Newfoundland for so many generations and Newfoundland as a society has existed for so long that surely we are Newfoundlanders. I can "kneel and say an *Ave*" at the grave of my great-great-great-grandfather, but it is not in Ireland: he lies in Newfoundland, at King's Cove, Bonavista Bay. The word "Newfoundlander" has been around at least since 1765, and people have been over-wintering in Newfoundland at least since 1610. We needn't think of ourselves, then, in terms of any mother country. My personal connection to the old sod is remote, yet how is it that when I read Frank McCourt's *Angela's Ashes,* the territory is so familiar – not the circumstances of his life, but the language and expressions and sense of place? How is it that Brian Moore's novels *The Luck of Ginger Coffey* and *Answer from Limbo* feel like my literature?

The startling discovery of my childhood was that the pope was Italian. How could that be, when the Church was Ireland incarnate? The dominant force in my childhood, perhaps greater than family, was church and convent school and in school, too, my world was truly Irish. The Presentation Sisters had arrived here in 1833. I fell in with them more than 125 years later, but only close sociological examination could tell if, in 1960, they were more Irish or more Newfoundland. Most of the sisters who taught me were Newfoundlanders but the convent they had entered at sixteen or seventeen, just out of school themselves, was closed. They went to work every day – teaching us – but did not go out for much else. They spent their lives in the order, moving around the network of convents scattered throughout the island. Visits home were rare, granted with dispensation if, for example, a family member were dying.

Part of our school was joined to the convent, and part was housed in the B.I.S., a five minute walk over the hill. Every morning a small flock of nuns crossed down. If one of them had to return to the convent during the day, we were sent along. Nuns did not go out in ones; they went in twos, or were accompanied by us, little girls whose only thought was what a privilege to walk Sister So-in-So up to convent square. The more I write about my childhood, the more sure I am that my brain was at least half dead. Or is it simply that way with childhood? A child takes everything in her or his stride and believes it normal. And perhaps the sight did seem normal enough to passers-by. As it is winter for most of the school year in Newfoundland, our school days were plagued with blustery winds and blowing snow. The convent square and church yard were windswept ice-fields, with no place to hold on. Turning the corner of the Basilica you were smacked with that familiar serum – wind, sleet and hail. This was before the Gap takeover of children's wear; kids march to school now in colourful clothing and funny hats, laden with bulging Barbie or Caillou backpacks, like soldiers in some curious army. We were bundled in drab woolen or cloth coats, woolen mitts, scarves, outside scarves, and brown gaiters that went over our shoes. A familiar sight would be two short old crones (us) anchoring a tall old crone – about thirty-five years old and wrapped in black – holding her down lest the St. John's winds and the laws of aerodynamics play upon her shawls and wimple and carry her out the Narrows. We felt responsible.

Girls (they did not come over as nuns) were still coming out from Ireland as late as 1911 to enter the convent in Newfoundland. One of the last of the Irish-born nuns was Mother de Sales. In the early 1880s, she had left her home in Tralee in County Kerry to come out and teach poor children in Newfoundland. During my childhood, she was still giving piano lessons in the convent parlour. On her one hundredth birthday she was carried out to the school and down the narrow staircase to the auditorium in the basement. There was an armchair, out of place in a sea of steel stacking chairs, waiting for her front row centre. Mother de Sales was eased into this humble throne, and we kids began to sing. We sang as if we ourselves had been born and raised in the streets of Limerick or Cork or Tipperary: "The Rose of Tralee," "The Young May Moon," "Bendemeer's Stream," "Danny Boy," "Believe Me If All Those Endearing Young Charms." And stashed in my memory are snatches of songs I've never heard since, like this vivid ditty which we sang with such credibility I thought I saw one of the older nuns look over her shoulder a few times:

> In a shady nook one moonlight night a leprechaun I spied,
> With scarlet cap and coat of green, a cruishkeen by his side,
> 'Twas tip-tap-tip his hammer went upon a weeny shoe,
> Annnnnd (*pause, wink, widen our eyes*) I laugh to think of the purse of gold,
> But the fairy is laughing too.

And we sang this tender Irish beauty:

> There is a Lady sweet and kind,
> Was never face so pleased my mind,
> I did but see her passing by,
> And yet I love her till I die.
>
> Her gesture, motion, and her smiles,
> Her wit, her voice, my heart beguiles,
> Beguiles my heart, I know not why,
> And yet I love her till I die.

What were her thoughts – this frail ancient woman shrunken inside her veil and wimple, lost and small in her massive robes? She sat there in this habit she'd lived in for eighty-four years, the heavy rosary and crucifix hanging off her belt, this young girl who at sixteen had stepped aboard a small vessel for a rough passage to a new land. She came to enter the Presentation Convent in Newfoundland, following the mission of its founder Nano Nagle. This gentle soul listened and watched from her chair. Were her mind or heart in County Kerry? Or was that world lost to her, after a lifetime in her new home? We rounded off our "gift" to her:

> You will never grow old, while there's love in your heart,
> Time may silver your golden hair, as you dream in your
>   old rocking chair;
> But keep our love in your heart, remember the times we
>   have known,
> And with our love in your heart, dear Mother, you will
>   never grow old.

Our daily speech was filled with non-standard expressions. We didn't say, "I've told her"; we said, "I'm after telling her." We said "ye" as the plural of you: "Are ye coming along?" "Did he say that overright her?" we would ask, meaning did he say it in her presence. It was "minding youngsters," not babysitting children, and "we'll see ye after tea," meaning supper. We used words like "rostrum," and when we were scolded, we were called "bold impellers," which seemed to mean we were a bad force. There was constant talk of "mortification." Our sentences were filled up with "poor soul" and "God rest his soul." If, on a sunny day, we saw a hearse in front of the church, we'd cheerfully mutter, "Happy is the corpse that the sun shines on." The same sight on a rainy day brought an equally cheerful "Happy is the corpse that the rain rains on." I haven't done the research, but I suspect these sayings came from Mother Ireland via Mother Redempta, Mother Borromeo, Mother Ursula. Like it or not, we were miniatures of old Irish women.

And was it President Kennedy's Catholicism or his Irish background (or perhaps the potent combination) that made him the hero of home and school? On that November day in 1963, we were in a large classroom after school, at glee club practice. The door flew open and our director appeared, flushed.

"On your knees, girls, President Kennedy's been shot. In the name of the Father and the Son and the Holy Ghost" and within seconds we were well into the Rosary, my crazy childish Catholic mind relieved that it was a Friday, allowing us to say the Sorrowful Mysteries. What if he'd been shot yesterday, a Joyful Mysteries day? Would we have said them, or would there have been a dispensation? Likely, Sister would have made the decision and worried about the consequences later. There was some relief in being a kid.

"The first Sorrowful Mystery, The Agony in the Garden: Our Father . . . " Sister Olivette intoned, and we fell into the well-known ritual. "Give us this day our daily bread."

We were wriggling through childhood under a heavy Irish shroud, but we never heard the word Ireland. I squint through the endless corridors of childhood memory; I squeeze my body tight trying to recall a reference. I block sound around me, trying to hear what Mother Aloysius is saying in front of the class, trying to read her lips, but Ireland is not there. No talk of County this or County that, no talk of north and south. The Troubles? They appeared much later in stark images in news magazines, but not in connection to us. Charles Stewart Parnell and his struggle for Home Rule? I learned of him later in ballads and songs. What of the famine – the failure of the potato crop that depopulated Ireland and drove the desperate to the new world? We knew about hungry children, but they were in pagan lands; if we saved enough mission money, they'd get food *and* a chance at eternal life. It's been more recently that St. John's has filled up with talk of Ireland. Local and imported scholars study the links between Newfoundland and Ireland: the immigration patterns, the dialect and accents, the traditional music of here and there. I went to school in a building owned and operated by the Benevolent Irish Society, and I was taught by nuns whose links to Ireland were real and recent, but of Ireland itself I knew nothing – except that many local boys went there to train as priests or doctors.

Was there a single Irish story in all our readers? Did we discover Daniel O'Connell and his efforts for the repeal of the union? Did we know about Robert Emmet's speech from the gallows, given as he died for Ireland? What of James Connolly storming the Dublin post office in 1916 and proclaiming the Republic of Ireland? *Nada*. What I know of Ireland I learned from literature, from Sean O'Casey's many volumes of memoir, from James Plunkett's *Strumpet City*, from James Joyce's *Ulysses*, from Yeats' *Autobiographies*, from Brendan Behan and Edna O'Brien, from the masterful storyteller William Trevor. From school, I recall dreary talk of Canada – reciprocity and car manufacturing and a town called Sault Ste. Marie. I remember a book with colourful child-heroes from many countries and continents, beginning with an African boy named Bunga, but I can't picture an Irish colleen, poet or patriot. The curriculum, likely beyond the control of the nuns, was barren of Ireland. I was twenty years old before I sat in a classroom and heard a single fact of Irish history, and that was in a university course on Irish literature.

Had I paid attention to the words of the songs I sang, I would have learned about Ireland, but I was vague and careless about texts. One of the many Irish songs I tinkled out countless times on the piano was "The Wearing of the Green." "Oh Paddy dear and did you hear . . . ," we chirped along as if it were a skipping song. I sang it with as much feeling and devotion to text as I would "Here we go round the Mulberry Bush." Now I listen to John McCormack sing that stirring ballad and can hardly believe my ears:

> O Paddy dear and did you hear the news that's going round?
> The shamrock is forbid by law to grow on Irish ground.
> No more St. Patrick's Day we'll keep, his colours can't be seen
> For there's a bloody law against the wearing of the green.
> I met with Napper Tandy and he took me by the hand,
> And he said, "How's poor old Ireland, and how does she stand?"
> She's the most distressful counterie that ever yet was seen,
> For they're hanging men and women for the wearing of the green.

The poet continues:

> When law can stop the blades of grass from growing as they grow,
> And when the leaves in summer-time their verdure dare not show,
> Then will I change the colour that I wear in my caubeen
> But till that day please God I'll stick to wearing of the green.

I weep now when I sing this song, thinking of the Irish denied nationhood in their own country, sometimes dying for their cause. The McCormack rendition I have is a 1912 recording made in New Jersey with a small studio orchestra conducted by Victor Herbert. The clarinets and trumpets pump out the accompaniment with indifferent cheerfulness as McCormack's high sweet tenor voice sings with passion and conviction. Songs lyrics, had I paid attention, could have taught me about Ireland.

One day a few years ago I was in a small outport in Conception Bay, in the home of an eighty-six-year-old man. With the exception of brief periods away for work, he had spent his life in this fishing community. His father and grandfather had known only this place. It was a grey Saturday afternoon in April. There'd been a funeral in the extended family earlier in the day, bringing the sons and daughters home from the city. The family was gathered in the living room, the youngest grandchild lying comfortably at his grandfather's feet, absorbed with colouring characters from *Star Wars*. Feisty political commentary and casual chit-chat criss-crossed the room. Outside, wet snow was falling. I sipped my brandy, felt the warmth. The hum of conversation ebbed a little and then a little more as we noticed one of the daughters holding up her hand to silence us. She flicked her head in the direction of her father. He was singing. He was staring into the distance, oblivious to all of us as the unfamiliar song filled the room. Snatches of lines and phrases were sputtering out, as if a tightly-locked memory had loosened a little. He sang in short phrases, the physical effort costing him; sometimes the line would fade out as if memory defeated him, then he would pick it up again somewhere later in the ballad.

The son sitting nearest me grabbed me.

"The '98 rebellion!"

The old man sang of cowards, of patriots, of brave sons, and a freed land as more and more of the ballad filled in. When he finished, his family stared at him in silence. They were used to him singing old songs, but not in recent years, and not this one. "Dad! Where did that come from?"

"Who taught you that?"

"It's the rebellion of 1798, the United Irishmen, Wolfe Tone and – "

The others cut off the excited academic son.

"What's it called?"

"Dad, did your father sing that?"

"I don't know." He beamed as if he'd caught the best fish on a poor trouting day. "I s'pose I must have heard it somewhere."

How long had it been lodged inside him? How much did he know of the story the ballad told? His father had died a young man, leaving not even a photo behind. None of these children had known their grandfather. It wasn't a culture that passed on mementos. It wasn't a culture with mementos to pass on. For the most part, households were lean; material goods were valued for their usefulness, not their sentiment. If the wood of a spare table could be put to better use as kitchen cupboards, then dismantle the table and make the cupboards. With many fishing families, where the sea matters more than the land, the legacy is often a package of skills and attitudes and the ingredients of oral culture.

A week later, a grey Saturday afternoon with more wet snow, the family was gathered again. They'd just buried their father in the cemetery across the road from his house. The song he had dredged up from ancient ancestral memory and sung for his children and grandchildren seemed a parting gift from their remote collective past, handed over four days before he died. The culture can be passed on less precariously now, with so much recorded music, and there are young people there ready to receive it. I've seen and heard the passion of John McCormack in a young Newfoundlander who's never set foot in Ireland. He's a handsome, cheerful young architect, just starting out in his career, and family life. He and his bride were hosting a housewarming in St. John's youngest suburb. The party was filled with the contagious optimism of the newly wed. Downstairs in the rec room, Kevin was playing Irish music for those who wanted to dance. He stood in front of the sound system and sang. There was no ego in his actions, nothing self-conscious; he didn't care if anyone was listening – he simply sang, as if the stories were so dear to him he had to. He sang "The Dutchman," "The Butcher Boy," "The Rising of the Moon," songs with lyrics like this, from "The Fields of Athenry":

> By a lonely prison wall
> I heard a young man calling,
> Nothing matters Mary when you're free;
> Against the famine and the crown
> I rebelled, they put me down.
> Now you must raise our child with dignity.

Upstairs, family and friends toured the house, teasing the bride about how soon "the baby's room" might be occupied. Downstairs, Kevin carried on singing, of dark-haired colleens and unrequited love, of pillage and plundering, of blood shed for a noble cause. He sang of national pride and national grief, and the nation was Ireland. He has never studied its history, never read an Irish book, yet he sang as if the culture and pain of the place were his. His knowledge, passion and love of Ireland have come to him through music.

I don't have these emotional connections to my Irish ancestry – except when I walk along Duckworth Street past the handsome building housing federal government offices in St. John's, the Humphrey Gilbert Building. Who, *exactly who,* suggested honouring an "Irish butcher" in this half-Irish town? Somebody who didn't read too far into Gilbert's biography. Nobleman, yes, Member of Parliament, yes, and great explorer. Read a little further and discover other accomplishments: the suppression and killing of hundreds of Irish. Gilbert didn't have much truck with the Irish – he said his dog's ears were too good to hear the speech of the noblest man among them. Armed with such healthy contempt, he was probably the right man for the job he was sent to do in 1566: quell rebellious Ireland and settle it with safe Devonshire gentlemen. He had his own way of doing business. When the Irish didn't hand over their lands and castles, he "would . . . win it per force, how many lives so ever it cost, putting man, woman and child of them to the sword." His boast, his words. To encourage smoother real estate deals, he lined the pathway to his camp with the heads of the executed. If an Irishman wanted to make a submission to Gilbert, he walked through a path lined on both sides with the heads of his own people. In Ireland, Gilbert was known as more devil than man; in England, he was knighted for his services. An odd choice for a St. John's hero!

A friend, an old man, once told me of an incident that took place at a cocktail party in St. John's in the 1970s. A young English doctor, newly arrived, ambition blazoned on his forehead, was welcomed generously. The women were offering to show his wife around town, and could someone help them find a house? During the evening, my friend overheard the new doctor talking to another Englishman who asked him his first impressions of Newfoundland.

He laughed.

"I'll be fine, I'm sure, but I think I've ended up with the bog Irish."

When he told me this story, twenty years later, my friend's eyes filled with tears. Not because we'd been called bog Irish, but because that doctor had stayed and made his way here, helped every step of the way by a community who never knew his contempt of them. That night, in my old friend's living room, I felt Irish.

My father was a modern man. He travelled to Egypt on his first honeymoon (my father married twice; I'm a child of the second marriage) in 1931. He travelled regularly by boat from St. John's to New York, and he once went to Vimy Ridge to kneel at the grave of his brother, a boy soldier who'd been killed there. My father's business links were with Wales, England, the United States and, briefly after Confederation, with Canada. He read contemporary literature such as Ayn Rand's *The Fountainhead* and Sinclair Lewis' *Babbitt*. He was firmly rooted in his native land and suffered no doubt or confusion about his nationhood – he was a Newfoundland patriot. But in the late 1930s, he made a hunt through Ireland for his ancestors, long before such journeys became a fashionable hobby.

I have my father's sketchy notebook from that trip. It is brown leather with a rich golden grain running through it. The cover is worn, but the gold embossed emblem of the stationer is still easy to read. If only he had known how few links would remain between us, how early he would die, surely he would have slowed down his careless scrawl. Even my mother, who prides herself on being able to read his writing, can only shrug at most of it. There are names and dates of people with surnames that belong to our family. I can read only two pages clearly. One is the draft of a telegram to Minnie Kelly of 6 Markland Street, Cheetham (?), Manchester.

"Will be in Manchester on my way to . . . Can I see you at station? G. Doyle."

There are a few inscriptions from graves, vaguely legible, amidst pages of scribbles and scrawls. Oh Dad! Why didn't you keep a proper journal, or at least write more neatly? Occasionally the scrawls reveal phrases from the inscription on a tombstone, like this: " . . . the passion of death in administering the last . . . solutions and religious to the belleaguered [sic] . . . members of the Dock during the . . . profession. He laboured without ceasing as a true minister of Christ and dispenser of the mysteries of God and in the end died a martyr to his personal zeal . . . was promoted to the parish of Dingle where after an incumbancy [sic] of 10 years he died on May 20 1849 . . . possession in an . . . Degree the spirit and virtues of his Sacred . . . "

The writing refers to Reverend Michael Devine, and the date 1865 hangs alone on a page of the notebook. He had been parish priest of Bareheaven(?). My father's mother was a Devine, but who was this man, and how was he related to us?

There is only one page in my father's notebook that is completely legible, carefully written as if the lazy writer at least began with good intentions. My notebooks are all the same – model penmanship on page one, a calligraphic mess by page three. His first page is perfect and reads:

    Poetical
    Musical
    Friendly
    <u>Easy Going</u>
    The Irish

My father returned to Ireland once, with my mother. There's a photo of them on horseback in the hills of Killarney. It *looks* as if they're having a good time, but was there something about that trip that turned my mother against the Irish? Years later, she took us on a three-month trek through Europe. In spite of her antipathy to Ireland, she felt she had to take us there.

"You won't like it, it rains all the time. And the Irish. Well, the *Irish* . . . " No elucidation was forthcoming from this woman whose Irish grandmother, on the Cape Shore of Newfoundland in the nineteenth century, spoke no English.

When it rained non-stop in Connemara, when tinkers hit upon us in Galway, when the tea was as cold and damp as the hotel rooms themselves, our mother would say only, "Hmph! Don't talk to me about the Irish."

The Irish, then, was one subject on which my parents disagreed. But my mother, like me, had been educated by the Presentation nuns, and her speech, like mine, was full of references to the old country. Her standard way of expressing quantity – of people, food, money – was "Enough to set old Ireland free." Thirty years later, I can't remove it from my own speech.

"So, how was the concert?" a friend will ask. "Did they get a crowd?"

I mean to say, yeah, they got a full house, but what comes out of my mouth is, "Enough to set old Ireland free."

When we were kids we rattled off Irish songs with no thought to their meaning. One was Thomas Moore's ballad of a mute harp, symbol of a silenced Ireland: "The harp that once through Tara's halls the soul of music shed/ Now hangs as mute on Tara's walls, as if that soul were fled."

> No more to chiefs and ladies bright the harp of Tara swells
> The chord alone that breaks at night, its tale of ruin tells
> Thus Freedom now so seldom wakes, the only throb she gives
> Is when some heart indignant breaks, to show that still she lives.

There was a mute harp in my childhood, too. It stood in the grand parlour in the convent, a testament to the ninety Irish girls – sisters, aunts, nieces, cousins – who spent their lives as Presentation Sisters in Newfoundland, passing on their love of music. Somewhere along the way it had grown silent, a symbol perhaps of the fogs of change that were stealing in. In the mid-1960s, we were told to no longer say we attended the convent; when the next batch of our scribblers was printed, they showed we were pupils of Presentation "School." With my turquoise cartridge pen, I scratched out "School" and continued to write "Convent" until I was forbidden to do so. Our schooling was becoming part of a new world – after all, we were, in theory anyway, schoolchildren in the modern country of Canada. Soon we would be up the road at the new high school where, on a September day in 1967, the first question asked of one thousand girls gathered in the auditorium was "Hands up, who's been to Expo 67?"

My Uncles Didn't Dance

One night, walking home from a choir rehearsal, I was going over in my head our conductor's new arrangement of the Newfoundland folksong "A Great Big Sea." She'd scored it for three-part female choir and piano. It's a catchy arrangement in a style welcome in classical choral repertoire. I thought again of the warring factions in the debate about Newfoundland music, the accusation that classical arrangements are an act of appropriation. I was still musing about this when I walked into my house, flopped on the couch and flicked on the TV.

Here was Great Big Sea, the high-energy Newfoundland "trad" group who take their name from the well-known folksong. They play traditional music in a contemporary style using guitar, mandolin, concertina, accordion, bodhran, tin whistle, bouzouki, fiddle, and button accordion. The boys are compelling; when you start to watch, you can't walk away. The leader, Alan Doyle (alas, no relation), is a supremely gifted performer. He's not like those pop icons who look like they're on duty tour – glum dudes too cool to smile. The look on Doyle's face is unabashed ecstasy, and it's infectious.

The crowd was wild – new light on the sober citizens of Ottawa! The show was from the civic centre, part of the GBS national Road Rage tour. Here was the traditional Newfoundland ballad "Jack Hinks" transmogrified, Jack with a new hard drive. It was like watching the Rolling Stones do "My Bonnie Lies Over the Ocean." The metre had been changed from its original 6/8, which gave the piece its gentle, rollicking sea shanty feel, to 2/4. The new metre and fast tempo drive the story of this "sea-faring, sail-making, gamboling, capering, grog-drinking hero – Jack Hinks." Syncopated bars disturb the metre to punch out certain lines: "we were bashed / on / the / rocks like hard / hunted / fox." In my head I could still hear Omar Blondahl and Alan Mills singing versions of this song, each of their recordings sounding like musical fireside chats – casual and chummy. I've sung it myself, too, hundreds of times, but this was like no Jack Hinks I had ever heard.

In the middle there's a wild accordion "break" based on a traditional Newfoundland tune. Back to a hale and hearty Jack, in the full thrust of life, having had a near miss in a storm at sea. Another change in metre – a few measures of a waltz this time – to tell us he'd been saved "by Providence kind, who so eases the wind, and on sailors so constantly thinks." At the end, even listening to the recording without the benefit of visuals, it's as if you can see Jack step forward, put out his hand and introduce himself with a nod and a wink. "Jack Hinks": the lead vocalist speaks rather than sings the last words, as is the way with many traditional singers. The piece concludes with a simple guitar chord. Jack's done.

That performance to my mind settled the debate of who's allowed to do what with "traditional" Newfoundland music.

Ah, Newfoundland music! I've spent my lifetime on both ends of this sticky spectrum. I have rolled around my living floor with tears in my eyes, laughing at the truly bizarre sounds emanating from mainland children's choirs singing "I'se the B'y." Yet I will go to my grave defending their right to take a folksong and do with it what they will. A folksong is up for grabs, but in Newfoundland there's a tight, snobbish circle who believe there is only one path of a folksong: it must be sung as it was traditionally sung. (There is little documentation to guide us here, however; it *is* an oral culture.) Preserving a piece of music as a museum piece or artefact is noble, and without that effort we might have lost our music, but when preservation moved into the territory of artistic tyranny, we arrived at a defining moment in the history of traditional Newfoundland music: *the great irony*. Purists holding fast to the notion that Newfoundland music belonged to the people removed the very democratic nature of it, laying out rules of who could sing a song, and how. The essence of the music was its accessibility: the music belonged to everyone. Songs were sung by the people, unaccompanied, or with the simple addition of a few instruments at hand, usually a fiddle or accordion. Ability to read music wasn't a factor as the songs were passed on orally. But when purists placed a defining stranglehold on the quintessential way to sing or perform a folksong, they did a cultural flip: they took ownership and made exclusions. An oboe player who knew his instrument was perfectly suited to a plaintive lament such as "She's Like the Swallow" was scoffed at: get out of here and stick to Haydn. There were no oboes in early Newfoundland! Determining that a school band sounded silly playing "The Sealer's Song" or that a choir singing "Petty Harbour Bait Skiff" in four-part harmony was laughable was contrary to the original spirit of traditional music. If you were a classically trained musician you dared not approach Newfoundland music; if you did, you were spoiling it. The response of the musical bullies was a definite and territorial Paws Off!

Choirs the world over sing rhythmically and harmonically sophisticated arrangements of their country's folksongs, as well as new works of art created from those melodies. There is no exclusivity. Take Joseph Canteloube. Just as well he wasn't a Newfoundlander. Canteloube was born in the Auvergne area of France in 1879. When he was a young man, he roamed around the Auvergne, seeking out authentic singers and hearing them sing the songs of the region. He wrote down the songs with care and accuracy and later published four volumes of them. These are folksongs, nonsense songs, playful love songs, pastoral songs, songs of the cuckoo. Out of these songs he made an imaginative and rich cycle of nine pieces set for soprano and piano (or soprano and orchestra), his colourful *Songs of the Auvergne*. In Newfoundland, such an activity before recent years was anathema. Young Joseph would have been dragged up to Gibbet Hill for his villainy, he and his manuscript flung into Deadman's Pond.

Bela Bartok composed challenging string quartets but he also spent his lifetime collecting the songs of his native Hungary. Beethoven and Haydn arranged and set Scottish folks songs. Antonin Dvorak worked the native music of his country, Czechoslovakia, into his art; when he lived in the United States, it was some of the indigenous music of that country – "what are called the Negro melodies," he said – that caught his ear. It's not uncommon for composers to fill up their music with the melodies and rhythms of their country. But when a Newfoundland song is arranged as a classical piece, there's a rolling of the eyes, a shaking of the head, a pained and worried look that suggests *all is now lost:* history, heritage, tradition, authenticity, gone – stolen by elitists.

But Newfoundland is a colony in recovery, and the desperate effort to retain our music in an authentic way is comprehensible to some extent. The new tyranny over folk music was part of a larger cultural despotism, and was a by-product of the neo-nationalism that awoke in the 1960s and '70s and centred around the notion that there was one "true" Newfoundland. There was a conception of this place fixed firmly in some minds that didn't allow for deviation, and it squeezed out much of the truth of our present as well as our past. Anything that fell outside the prescribed defining characteristics of "Newfoundland culture" was heresy. Newfoundland meant outport, it meant fishing, it meant poor fisherfolk; everything else was false. And here's the thing: this bullying assertion, this putting forward and giving value to all things outport, was a natural, understandable, and *probably necessary* corrective to the fact that the arts and Newfoundland culture had fallen into odd hands. It was difficult to find Newfoundlanders in positions of influence in what's broadly called the "cultural sector." Brits and Brit-wannabes – Newfoundlanders who'd never crossed the ocean but who had English accents – tended to fill positions in the arts, in the provincial arts and culture centres, in local amateur theatre, in groups dedicated to "the folk arts," at CBC Radio, even in the Faculty of Arts at Memorial University.

There's a tale told of a talented CBC television producer, a Newfoundlander, who turned to his colleagues one day and said, "Come on, boys, let's go down to Quidi Vidi [the closest cove to St. John's harbour] and go out in a boat so we can sail in through the Narrows" – an allusion to the belief that Newfoundlanders were often passed over for jobs and promotions in the cultural arena, in favour of those from away.

When I was a student at Memorial University in 1974, there was a plan that on March 31 (the twenty-fifth anniversary of the "feast of Confederation," as we mockingly called it), Newfoundlanders working in the areas that housed the humanities departments would go to work that day with their faces blackened with shoe polish, taking a page from John Howard Griffin's experiment described in *Black Like Me*. It was a fantasy because Newfoundland consciousness was not high enough for significant participation, and the plan was too hard to execute with so few conspirators. (A plot I was *not* part of was to blow up Pearson's Peak. Happily, the patriot in that case was visited by a heavy dose of good sense and he nixed the idea himself a few days before.) There were exceptions, but our scheme would have made a statement as the "white" professors from away and the "black" cleaners and administrative staff (Newfoundlanders) went about their business. Our motivation was a frustration born of sitting passively in front of professors who daily expressed contempt for us. After years of living and teaching in Newfoundland, some still refused to pronounce the name of the place as we did, holding on to some colonial version they'd learned before they came over. One Oxbridge professor, unable to accept where he'd ended up, regularly gave himself away; he said "here" when he spoke of England, "there" when he spoke of the new world.

This colonialism was the fertile breeding ground for young Newfoundlanders waking up to a Newfoundland consciousness or nationalism in the '70s, a period described by Sandra Gwyn as a renaissance in Newfoundland art. The support, money and performance opportunities for most music and theatre were under the control of a "director of cultural affairs," a position and title reminiscent of minor functionaries in Gilbert and Sullivan's Titipu. Around the real and symbolic figures of cultural power, there grew up indigenous theatre collectives like CODCO and The Mummers Troupe, and the groundbreaking band Figgy Duff. Things happened quickly and soon there was a much-needed reversal in who "owned" Newfoundland culture, but there was one unfortunate piece of fall-out: the baby that went out with the bath water was classical music. Not native, not indigenous, it was dismissed as part of a culture that had been imposed on us and, in the minds of some, had nothing to do with us. It was shoved out from the canon of acceptable Newfoundland artistic activity. Perhaps it has something to do with a weird sense we have of ourselves: there is something laughable about singing our songs in a certain way, as if the songs – or perhaps we ourselves – are not worthy of such fanciness.

For my own part, I was in something of an unusual position. I was urban, and around that time in Newfoundland, you could scarcely qualify as a Newfoundlander if you were from St. John's. There were narrow definitions about what a real Newfoundlander was; all of a sudden pedigrees from outports were sought and touted up. One university professor from a small community on a remote coast showed up at Memorial University speaking with a British accent. Within a year or two, the carefully nurtured affectation was dropped; he threw off his loafers and started teaching class in his rubber boots. Outport was in, and the more legitimate your claim to this heritage, the more of a *real* Newfoundlander you were.

My parents were both from small outports, but in my childhood we had no connection with their places of origin. My four grandparents had died before I was born. My mother's family had long moved from her birthplace, and her seven siblings had left Newfoundland. There was no one remaining on my father's side who retained a connection to his birth place, not even my dad, who died when I was three. So the outport in my childhood, despite my parents' background, was a remote concept. (My mother did take me around during the summers to see outport Newfoundland. She taught me to respect the life and work of a fishing community, forbidding the word "bayman," a derogatory term for an outharbourman, in our house.) I was surrounded in school by girls who went to their grandmothers for weekends, who went "around the bay" for the whole summer, who were part of huge extended families. Whenever I phoned a classmate to chat about school or homework, there was an aunt or uncle in the background, someone there for dinner, or there to mind them because their father was away or their mother was ill. It looked awfully rosy in there, through the collective window of my girlfriends' homes. I was from a family short on home life, for my brothers were always away at boarding school or in the seminary or married. I had no uncles who danced. My great-uncles, all dead, had been writers, folklorists, balladeers, publishers. I had to walk in shame during those delicate years, was scarcely a Newfoundlander at all in the Nazi-Newfie kingdom of the late '60s and the 1970s.

Yet I was a dedicated Newfoundland nationalist, ready to walk in the parade that would lead us out of Confederation. I was the gofer for my brother Bill, carting gear around the island as he made his ironic film *Pure Silver,* celebrating the twenty-fifth anniversary of Newfoundland's entry into Confederation. I behaved suitably outrageously to actors who were imported from away to work in local theatre groups. (I was, however, extremely polite to Rick Salutin, a Toronto playwright who arrived around this time to assist local theatre collectives.) And I felt like an undercover agent, toiling by day for Joey Smallwood as a writer and researcher for his *Book of Newfoundland*, knowing, with the certainty and purity of youth, that my healthy clear-minded anti-confederate stance was the right one: Smallwood had screwed Newfoundland. I had ended up, that summer, working for him accidentally. He had called the university asking for suggestions for a recent grad who could do the work and I was recommended. He was a good employer, he paid well, and there was no job I could have been happier with, but I was aware of the double nature of my life.

At that time Mr. Smallwood's "office" was the second floor of a private home on Forest Road in the east end of St. John's. He worked in the master bedroom and my space was an open area adjacent to the main door, so that I saw the few visitors who came and went. I had heard Mr. Smallwood's voice on the radio probably twenty times a day my whole life; his voice and image had dominated Newfoundland until his defeat in 1971-72. This remote demigod, this bogeyman of my childhood, was now a small, funny-looking man, casually dressed in slippers and a silk lounging jacket, working about ten yards from me. I felt like Dorothy when the wizard came out from behind the curtain. We had daily "meetings." I didn't say a word, just scribbled in my notepad how many print inches I was to write about each subject in the biography section. It was *the* summer of anti-confederate sentiment among the young, because of the twenty-fifth anniversary, and here I was working with the enemy.

A greater irony was Joey's own position, for this "Father of Confederation" was shunted aside during the celebratory year because his Liberal party was no longer in power. He was a Newfoundland patriot in his own way, attempting a monument to Newfoundland's past with his book. I was a daily witness to Joey burying himself in his work as the grand party went on around him. A loyal band of supporters tried to cobble together a small corner of it for him, a parallel celebration, but it was the poor man's feast. A dinner was planned for a school auditorium in Conception Bay. Around the office, it was assumed I would go. My whole summer was spent in the anti-confederate underground; now here I was expected to attend a dinner honouring this icon of Confederation!

At that time, I lived in jeans and work boots, making exceptions for wakes and funerals. I drove to Bay Roberts and, in the parking lot of the school, squatting in my green Datsun hatchback, I struggled into a bra, skirt and blouse, nylons and dressy shoes, an impostor on many fronts as I walked into the school auditorium. I couldn't say no. Yes, he was former Premier J.R. Smallwood, he was the "only living Father of Confederation," he was the focus of all my anger about Newfoundland's loss of nationhood – before I met him. Now, he was my tolerant employer who treated me well, called me "Miss Doyle," and picked me up once when I was hitchhiking. He was also an old man, left out of the best party in town, a party celebrating the event he created. He was like a puzzled husband refused admittance to his own anniversary dinner. He had been a tough, fierce, ruthless politician, yet at some level he did not understand this turn of events. There was a naïve streak in him – perhaps a romancing brought about by age. He was hurt.

This, then, was my day job that infamous summer. My night job was sitting in Bridgett's Pub, being cynical, ranting and roaring about Confederation, and sewing miniature Newfoundland flags (the Pink, White and Green) on my knapsack. If we'd known about body piercing, we would have adorned ourselves with symbols of our "secret nation." I hung out with the actors my roommate, Maddy Williams, worked with as they toured the island with their "pageant," moved by the sight of the sealers left on the ice to die, startled by the young actor who knelt and bared her breasts ("She's some brazen." "She's from Tronto.") as Mary March, one of the last of the Beothucks, is said to have done to reveal her womanhood to her captors.

I was a patriot, a nationalist, but I was separated from the crowd by one thing: music. It was as if wanting to play Haydn trios was an act of treachery. In Britain, Fairport Convention and Steeleye Span were playing "traditional" music in a way that was not traditional. They took this music and did with it what they would. They incorporated the instruments, techniques and style of rock and pop and contemporary folk. Now in Newfoundland suddenly it was acceptable, even cool – *fabulous* – to move away from the traditional. Drums and electric guitars and basses were allowed. Amplification was in, everything was in, *except* a classical treatment of Newfoundland music, and classical music itself.

Yet what is the difference between a folk song arranged for string quartet or choir or concert band, and the same song arranged for and played by a rock band? And here's where the argument for retaining music as it was sung falls apart for me, for what emerges is not a purist trying to preserve music as it was, but a cultural despot defining what is permitted, selecting and excluding. Granted, the musicians of Figgy Duff were clever and imaginative in their arrangements of Newfoundland music while Toronto composer Howard Cable was not. But if those who were interested in traditional music had been open-minded, there would have been more forays into classical composition and arrangement, and this field would have grown. Instead, the door was shut. Classical music was shunted aside and its practitioners made to feel awkward and unwelcome at a time when traditional musicians, poets, painters, actors and writers were coming into their own. Music had been taught in schools in Newfoundland more than drama or visual art or creative writing, and there had been many more choirs than drama clubs or visual arts classes. It is sad that in Newfoundland, where music is the art most enjoyed and practised by most people, the art form that has lagged farthest behind is the composition and arrangement of classical music.

The Newfoundland songs I first heard and sang were from a collection published by my father. In the 1920s, he had begun to write down the songs he heard in his travels around outport Newfoundland. He was in trade – manufacturing cod liver oil, distributing patent medicines and household products – and visited his customers personally, going about by boat. He persuaded the Canadian, American and British companies he represented to buy ads and, in 1927, published *Old-Time Songs and Poetry of Newfoundland*. As he gave out the books free, they ended up in most Newfoundland households. On one page there was a song, on the opposite page a picture of the product he was advertising. It was a brilliant idea of a man ahead of his time, and it was the work of a patriot. My father believed the story of a country was as likely to be found in its songs as in its formal records and documents. He prefaced his introduction with this epigraph: "Let me make the Songs of my Country and I care not who makes the Laws." (Later, in the 1950s, he suggested publicly that every child in Newfoundland spend part of the school day singing our songs; this would give them greater joy later in the music "of their country," and "add something worthwhile to their accomplishments.")

That first collection (and his 1940 and 1955 editions) was a rich mix of songs about disasters at sea, sealing, love won and love lost, the Newfoundland railway, and politics. One song came out of the 1869 election fought largely on the issue of confederation with Canada. "The 'Antis' of Plate Cove" was written by Mark Walker, the talented Bonavista Bay songwriter from Tickle Cove, a community not too far from Plate Cove.

> And now to conclude this short ditty:
> I hope a good lesson we've taught
> And touters sent here from the city
> Have learned that Plate Cove can't be bought.
> Our fathers came here to get freedom
> Their sons will not barter away;
> Then hurray for the "Antis" of Plate Cove
> The "Athens" of Bonavist Bay.

Sometimes the songs related an incident or described a "time" (soiree), such as the party – and even the cake – immortalized in this song:

> There was glass-eyes, bull-eyes and fresh butter,
> Lampwicks and liniment too,
> Pastry as hard as a shutter,
> That a billy goat's jaw couldn't chew;
> Tabacco [sic] and whiskers of crackies,
> That would give you the fever and ache
> You'd crack off from the knees if you happen to sneeze
> After eating this *Trinity Cake*.

Most of these songs and ballads were a hair's breadth from disappearing in our precarious oral culture. The collection saved them and popularized them, moving the songs around an island where the population lived in isolated communities along the coast. Songs could have been well-known in one area and unknown in another. Publishing them validated the music sung around the island at home, at work, at play.

These were the songs I grew up with. In our house, when I was very young, Newfoundland songs were played on piano and on piano accordion by a talented group of my father's friends and his cousins. Traditional dancing, the fiddle, the button accordion, and the kitchen party were not part of my tradition. No dancing uncles. My father came from a line of balladeers and writers. His mother's brothers included Maurice Devine (founding publisher of the newspaper *The Trade Review*) and P.K. Devine, whose work includes *Devine's Folk Lore of Newfoundland in Old Words, Phrases and Expressions* (1937). Another uncle, John Valentine Devine, wrote one of the best known Newfoundland ballads, "The Badger Drive."

My father himself wrote songs and parodies, including "The Merchants," "A Noble Fleet of Sealers" (sung to the tune of "The Old Polina") and, in the late 1940s, more than one anti-confederate ballad. "All Gone Now" blamed Confederation for the scarcity of rabbits on the Bonavista Peninsula in the early '50s. He also wrote a parody of "The Cat Came Back." This tells the tale of the cat who

Bob McLeod (left) and Nish Rumboldt, two well-known Newfoundland musicians, were part of the group of my father's friends and cousins who gathered at our home for musical evenings.

survives many attempts on her life. In my father's version, the cat is taken on various Newfoundland adventures: she is dynamited, she is put on a train going west, she's dropped from a plane over Baccalieu Island and she's sent to the ice (the seal hunt):

> Gave her to John Blackmore to take out to the ice
> And drown her in a bobbin'-hole, which wasn't very nice,
> But the crew they couldn't find her though they searched
>   in all their bunks,
> For the cat she ran ashore one night and crawled upon the
>   Funks.

And on it goes until:

> The cat lay by the radio and dreaming one fine day,
> When someone turned on CBC and it began to play;
> The cat she looked around a bit and then she raised her
>   head,
> And when they played *O Canada*, the cat dropped dead.

At the time that Newfoundland's nationhood was being voted on, and then voted out, my father was producing for general distribution professional recordings of Newfoundland songs. He hired a male vocal studio quartet in Toronto to make recordings, privately produced by RCA, of "Tickle Cove Pond," "The Sealer's Song," "The Hardy Sealers," "The Badger Drive," and "The Old Polina." He gave these out to customers and friends. They have almost completely disappeared. A few years ago, I got a phone call from a man who told me he was leaving Newfoundland for good – his children had settled out west. His house was on the market and he was holding a sale for much of his valuable pre-confederate Newfoundlandia. There was something he wanted me to have, if I would come by.

I went to the home of this stranger, feeling sick that the age-old need for work had not only driven his children from Newfoundland, but this retired generation as well.

"Your father gave this to my father," he said, and passed me a homemade wooden box, a few inches bigger and thicker than a long-playing record. The back of the box was a solid piece of wood, the front consisted of four or five slats, as if ends of wood had been salvaged to make this case. The whole thing was held together by screws. On the box in blue ink was written: "Two Gramaphone (*sic*) Records of Nfld Songs. Given me by Gerald S. Doyle, 1948. To open, unscrew [arrows point to the left and right]."

The labour, the care, that had gone into the casing! This man's father had built a housing for the records, too precious to trust to a paper sleeve. I know of many beloved recordings, but I have never seen a box built to hold a record. I was moved, too, to think of the moment between the two men in this house, a few hundred yards from the Colonial Building, the seat of government, in the same year that the country of Newfoundland voted itself out of existence. On the morning of April 1, 1949, Newfoundlanders woke in their new country of Canada, but no one owned their souls. My father carried on with his own gestures and expressions of patriotism. The extraordinary recordings of the Commodore's Quartet were one small part of that. These close harmony arrangements sung by the musical and hearty voices of the Commodore's Quartet are as untraditional and as remote from Newfoundland as you can get – and they are my favourite arrangements of Newfoundland songs.

My father was unusual. He wasn't an academic, or a professional musician, or a folklorist coming from away to study us. He was a businessman, and he was at the very early days of collecting Newfoundland songs. I love the fact that the songbooks were tied up with the promotion of his business, but business wasn't cool in the 1970s when traditional music was on the rise in Newfoundland. Gerald S. Doyle and the song books were dismissed, not by the people, but by a small crowd of the ascendancy in the traditional music scene. The criticism sometimes levelled against the songbook was that it was a collection of well-known songs. (This brings to mind Yogi Berra's comment about a certain club: no one goes there anymore because it's too crowded.)

In 1990, Newfoundland producer Kelly Russell asked some of our best musicians to choose a well-known Newfoundland song and record it as they liked. This CD, *Another Time*, opened up the possibilities of new treatments of familiar songs in a way that was acceptable to the musicians in the "trad" music scene. *Another Time* presents twelve traditional Newfoundland songs, mostly from the Doyle songbook, in non-traditional ways – blues, wonderful saxophone playing wandering around familiar melodies, Latin rhythms, a Caribbean flair to "Jack Was Every Inch a Sailor." There's even what I would call a chamber music scoring of "Tickle Cove Pond," with fiddle, guitar, cello and a keyboard sounding something like a harp. Ron Hynes sings this sweet song with its quintessential moment in Newfoundland music, describing how and why a song might be written to preserve a story or incident. The song tells of a man coming home from the woods with a load of firewood in the spring of the year. On this particular day, Kit, his mare, warns him not to take the shortcut across the pond; the ice is too thin.

> I knew that the ice became weaker each day,
> But still took the risk and kept hauling away,
> One evening in April, bound home with a load,
> The mare showed some halting against the ice road
> And knew more than I did, as matters turned out,
> And lucky for me had I joined in her doubt.
> She turned 'round her head, and with tears in her eyes,
> As if she were saying: "You're risking our lives."
>
> All this I ignored with a whip-handle blow,
> For man is too stupid dumb creatures to know
> The very next minute the pond gave a sigh,
> And down to our necks went poor Kitty and I.

He called for help and two reliable families, the Oldfords and Whites, came along. Then the vignette that captures the songwriter on the spot:

> When the bowline was fastened around the mare's breast
> William White for a shanty song made a request.
> There was no time for thinking, not time for delay.
> So straight from his head came this song right away:
>
> Lay hold William Oldford, lay hold William White,
> Lay hold of the hawser and pull all your might,
> Lay hold of the bowline and pull all you can"
> And with that we brought Kit out of Tickle Cove Pond.

Great Big Sea's "Jack Hinks" makes the argument that good musicians can take a traditional song and do with it what they will. So does Joseph Petric and Guy Few's recording of Newfoundland music arranged by Andrew Huggett. I don't believe in ownership or exclusivity. Jim Joyce has recorded "Hard, Hard Times," a straightforward but beautiful arrangement of perhaps our best ballad, with plaintive commentary from the harmonica. The same song was recorded by Ron Hynes and the Wonderful Grand Band, a powerful and moving, but entirely different, rendition of this great song. For every pebble on the beaches of Newfoundland, there's a professionally mastered recording, a homemade cassette, or simply someone singing somewhere. We're all at it. The field is wide and includes jazz, country, blues, bluegrass, composed songs – like Ron Hynes' "St. John's Waltz" and his "Atlantic Blue" – as well as classical arrangements such as D.F. Cook's challenging (to the singers, not to the audience) "Lukey's Boat," his tender "The Morning Dew," and Valerie Long's moving setting for female choir of "Drowsy Sleeper," a gem she found in the Greenleaf and Mansfield collection *Ballads and Sea Songs of Newfoundland.*

If I were walking through the casbah in Morocco I would recognize the sound of a Newfoundland accordion player, and don't tell me there hasn't been one there. I know for sure that Newfoundland repertoire was once played for hours on a blazing hot afternoon in Crete on a sweet sounding concertina purchased in Athens. The lonely musician and her friend entertained themselves to ward off death by heat exhaustion, as buses to everywhere except their destination regularly passed by. (I've since purchased a dictionary with the Greek alphabet; next time I want the bus to Iraklion, I'll recognize Ιράκλιον.)

Newfoundlanders are lucky: we are a people with a huge repository of music rich in stories, characters and humour; songs of nostalgia, of loss, of the fearsome sea, of the beauty of the land. It's an integral and unifying part of us. Music gathers the Newfoundland diaspora when Buddy Wasisname and the Other Fellers and other talented groups criss-cross the country. Tens of thousands of people come out to see them, and sing with them. On the CD *100% Pure,* the audience (Ottawa again!) joins in for "Song for Newfoundland." There is no dispute here, musical or otherwise, in the spontaneous singing by the unofficial choir, that lonesome band of exiles:

> She's a rocky isle in the ocean,
> She's pounded by wind and by sea,
> You may think that she's rugged and cold,
> But she's home sweet home to me.

The March of My Soul

I wasn't a normal teenager. While other girls were drooling over glossy magazines about hair and lipstick, I lay on my bed watching the youth of America march across the pages of *Instrumental* magazine. There they were in their splendid red uniforms with brass buttons, little soldiers of John Philip Sousa. The brisk rat-a-tat-tat of the snare drum kept their steps lively, their spirits high, and the steady thud of the bass drum marked their pace. I could hear the stirring music cheering the football team to glory or calling the patriots to war. The fat mellow tuba helped the bass drum, the trombones and euphoniums punched out the harmonies while rows of clarinets and trumpets competed for the melody. And above it all, soaring out over the fields, out across the pages of the magazine and right into my bedroom in downtown St. John's was the piccolo, weaving higher and higher above the others, ornamenting the melody with descants and trills.

My earlier pact with the devil – no talking in school in exchange for membership in the Vienna Boys Choir – was off, as the devil had not kept her part. Now I would try again: anything, anything to be part of that world, right there in the centrefold. I wanted the colourful lanyards, the high boots, the bobby's hat with ribbons and swirls smartly tucked under my chin. I wanted to be in that uniform, marching, marching around those big lush American fields in a country where, it seemed, the sun always shone.

Alas, the closest I came was peeking out from under the railing around the grassy campus at my brothers' school. Sports Day closed off every year, the first week in June. Every boy in the school was out: the younger ones in white shorts and white collegiate pullovers, the older ones with gold stripes sewn down the legs of their grey trousers, sporting school ties and matching peaked cadet caps. They marched up and down the huge field, precision marching, spelling out the name of the school, the pope's name and other relevant data. From the age of four or five, I watched with envy as my older brothers participated in this spectacular military orgy. Trained by a retired military captain, they drilled again and again until the product was elaborate, colourful and, yes, beautiful. But this school and its glories were for boys. In my year-end concerts, I played piano duets with other little girls and, as we got older, sat demurely in long white cotton dresses with pink ribbon sashes, sawing our way through "Snow White Fantasy" and other girlish repertoire. I kept my own fantasy alive.

I was an unlikely recruit at the Royal Newfoundland Regiment. I was eighteen, the first woman ever to turn up for a band audition. I had long hair that hadn't been combed in a week, jeans with coloured flowers embroidered on the legs, and a navy blue poncho. But they needed a piccolo player and I was their man. Besides, uniform and dress code would take care of any deviance on my part, although the uniform did prove problematic. The Canadian military had just changed over to a fairly attractive suit, much like that worn by airline personnel, but the band, having had no call to order women's uniforms, had nothing for me. Eventually I was issued a khaki jacket and long skirt, a hospital-green stiff-collared shirt, black tie, and a boxy hat that offered options needed in certain war zones: netting, turn-down ear flaps and a peak that protruded about five inches in front of me. Private Doyle was dressed.

Musicians in marching bands read their music from miniature music stands that screw into their instruments, but these lyres don't work on piccolos because the instrument extends horizontally. The contemporary solution is a discreet lyre that straps on the left wrist, like a watch strap. But in my day, it was still the Boer War relic: an ancient wooden snake that began under the right arm, crooked around the back, hooked under the left armpit and poked its head

The Royal Newfoundland Regiment Band with its first female member, in Bowring Park, St. John's, c. 1973. (Photo courtesy of Marina Adams)

up in front. It was heavy, made of hardwood about three inches wide, and smelled of every school desk I'd ever sat in. To hold it, let alone march with it, was a feat – the lyre and uniform weighed me down about twenty-five pounds. But the peaked hat and serpentine lyre provided the cover I needed to be involved in military activities in those heady hippie times.

Because at that time to be associated with anything to do with the military was taboo. It was the era when, passing cadets outside the grocery store selling poppies, we would glare at the scrubbed young innocents and snap, "We don't support the military." To sustain being in the band while the rest of my life was "alternative" required the conspiracy of my housemate. On band nights, we would plant my clothes in a little room off the back porch. I'd creep in through the back door in full military regalia and switch uniforms, exchanging my war khakis for faded jeans and tie-dyed t-shirt. All this, and more devious lying and sneaking when the band left town to be "on parade" in some other community – all this for the thrill of marching in formation, filled with the joy of Sousa, letting my piccolo ring out over the hilly streets, harbours and wharves of Newfoundland.

I came close to discovery once when my boyfriend turned up at the War Memorial as a silent protester, dressed in jeans and a denim jacket with a huge peace symbol on the back. He was standing about five feet from me and, although two hours before we'd been enveloped in an intimate pose after a night of passion, he didn't recognize me. I felt a twinge of conscience wondering if playing the piccolo in a military band while professing pacifism constituted cheating on a lover.

I was the odd man out in the band, the guys often going into the back room to tell guy jokes. I was the odd man out, too, when the chap sitting next to me suddenly realized why I always had matchboxes stored with my cigarette papers. (We used the papers for cleaning the pads of our keys.) But I wasn't foolish enough to smoke up on the base and he, a conservative middle-aged man, was good enough to keep my secret.

And so in those years I marched. I loved the upbeat marches we would play, the wickedly difficult passages from von Suppé's *Light Cavalry Overture,* the teasing piccolo part in "Stars and Stripes Forever." I marched on Labour Day, marched on November 11 and, most of all, marched on July 1st – July Drive in Newfoundland – the day we commemorate the brutal battle of Beaumont Hamel. Part of the 1916 Somme Offensive in World War I, this was a real and symbolic blow to the Newfoundland Regiment – mown down in four minutes. It was the moments standing at the War Memorial that I will always recall. Standing in the shadow of the monument to Newfoundland's war dead, we played Handel's mournful "Dead March" from *Saul,* an unofficial anthem of the RNR band. The sombre pulse of the lower brass and the muffled drum begin this piece, then layers of instruments are added slowly until the music swells, and the feeling swells. Our band played out for all to hear, out over the crowds standing up and down the steps and all around the sides of the monument, the strains of the music floating above the pilot dock below and out across the harbour to boats which stop and wait to hear this annual vignette, this moment when we say, collectively, we will not forget. We will not forget the part we played, such a sacrifice for a remote war. And now the band is playing full and the glory of war is gone and there is nothing left except a sense we should not have had to undergo such loss, the tiny nation that we were, caught up in a war removed from us.

And somehow, in the midst of all this memory, a tradition has grown that we remember others, too – men lost in battles closer to home, battles not of humankind's making. The monument itself honours not just the soldier and sailor, but the Newfoundland woodsman and fisherman as well. We turn to the hymn associated with the great sealing disasters, and remember those who perished on the ice, and I want to put down my instrument now and sing, sing with the lone voices starting up here and there among the crowd, I want to be part of this unofficial choir singing:

> Eternal Father! strong to save, whose arm doth bind the restless wave,
> Who bidd'st the mighty ocean deep its own appointed limits keep
> Oh, hear us when we cry to thee for those in peril on the sea!

But my place is to play, and we carry on accompanying the wreath layers as they, with their own rhythm, perform their rituals, some in uniform, some not, some quite young, and some so old we know their grief is personal. My eye falls on one man, behind the iron fencing, close enough I see a tear, a tear he lets remain. He stands apart, like a private mourner at a public funeral. He wears three poppies; for him, "the fallen" have names. I turn away.

In November, too, we come here, November with its frosty nip coming off the water. When I can, between pieces, I steal a look at the stolid face of the trumpeter who sounds "The Last Post," at children lost inside mounds of snowsuit whimpering from the cold and demanding to be shoved higher on their parents' shoulders to see more. There are politicians in their immaculate navy wool coats, and old men shivering because they don't have the right clothes to stand still for an hour in such temperatures. We march off, our fingers now frozen against our silver and brass instruments, the crowd dispersing, kids contentedly returned to the warmth of cars, couples looking for the nearest hot coffee. Passing by, an hour later, the scene has changed; the downtown is empty. The only signs that we were here are the wire wreath stands blowing about with their bursts of colour brightening the drab November Day. All still.

This part of my musical year is marked off once again. Home I go to sneak into the back porch, do the quick change and join a bunch of friends sprawled around the living room floor, smoking, nodding and gently bopping as John Lennon pleads from the stereo, "Give Peace a Chance." I inhale, a deep satisfying draw, hold it as long as I can and exhale slowly, controlling the air stream as a piccolo player would, content with the various private parts of me.

On Poplar Avenue

A friend once told me that the first morning after she left home, she took a shower at 4:00 a.m. She set her alarm, woke up and did it *because she could*, with no one to comment, complain, or ask why. I left home after third-year university and my first act was to turn on the stereo, turn *up* the stereo, and let those riffs and quarter notes roam free.

Poplar Avenue wasn't a natural next step from living at home. There'd been a limbo, a half-way stop, introduced by my brothers. I see myself tentatively entering the squatty hall of my brothers' pad, a wary convent girl affecting nonchalance as suspicious foreign scents came out to greet me; even the incense was unidentifiable, mixed as it was with curry and pot. My brothers showed me around. In the kitchen, tofu this, "soya" that and gangling white worms sprouting in gauze-covered jars. Dope, I thought, but on my next visit the stuff turned up on my salad plate, introduced as mung bean sprouts. I followed one brother and his girlfriend tentatively as they parted strings of hanging beads to pass through to the living room. I tried to avert my eyes from the double mattress on the floor. I was chatty, in a nervous kind of way, covering up my horror and filled with a strong sense that *Mom wouldn't want me here, my brothers are off the rails*. What had happened to the seminarians who'd come home for Christmas and ask me, with a solicitude beyond their years, how glee club was coming along? To brothers who'd sit on the piano bench next to me and play the other girl's part so I could practice my duet of "Angels We Have Heard on High"?

"Listen to this," one brother said now, easing a record from its sleeve onto the turntable, and in that moment life tilted a little. *"Sweet Sir Galahad came in through the window in the night when the moon was in the yard,"* sang the clear lyrical voice of Joan Baez, roaming easily around the story she was telling. Weren't there only two kinds of music, classical and junk? We listened to one album after another: Pete Seeger, Bob Dylan, Leonard Cohen. I had never listened to a record *with* anyone before. *"I've looked at life from both sides now,"* Joni Mitchell's sweet lilt filled the room. My other brother picked up a bass guitar that was lying on the floor and started playing along on Carole King's raunchy "It's Too Late." I sipped what I thought was liquid marijuana (I had never seen tea leaves or a tea-ball before) and began the slow drift into a warm new place. I left that day with Bob Dylan's *John Wesley Harding* under my arm and a copy of *Small is Beautiful* in my jacket pocket. The brothers, my rescue team, had grabbed me from the slippery slide of going to my grave a Holy Heart girl, a teacher in a parochial elementary school, driving kids around in a minivan. Still, I kept one foot on the mother track.

Then my mother went to Labrador.

I had sailed out through the St. John's Narrows with her, then pleaded ill, got off at the first port, and hopped into my brothers' waiting van. Home Alone. And while she took her trip, I took mine: that first memorable days-long psychedelic adventure of all-night television with Joey Smallwood and Fidel Castro, Pink Floyd, the Virgin Mary and my father's soul all appearing and disappearing. The "event" culminated on Signal Hill with me pouring my stoned crazy self into the hard bore of my metallic flute, shivering in the cool dawn, all for my brother's Super 8 movie camera. Where did the music come from? It was not the Handel sonata I was working on, nor the Bach suite. The music came from some unknown interior zone.

By that time, I was living upstairs in the tiny room I inherited when the last of the brothers moved on. Downstairs, the hi-fi sat in the living room like a bulky steamer trunk on legs, spilling out the Mitch Miller Singers or the soundtrack of *The Music Man*. Upstairs was for serious listening. Here was the latest gear: a true sound system with components, wires crawling high and low, the speakers positioned to produce perfect stereo. My mother, who had remodelled an old home in a glamorous way, had unwittingly provided a perfect environment for teenage lifestyle: there was a balcony off this second-storey bedroom which allowed for enhanced listening, without the fear of a peculiar sweet-smelling smoke drifting into the downstairs. After a short stint there, I got my own place and the listening room grew: an entire house was open to jazz, blues, rock, folk and classical. Country and western came later, in the love-pain package.

Anything went on Poplar Avenue so that the words recall not an address or a street where I lived, but a state of mind, a time-out between a tight childhood and responsible adulthood. It was a five-year event, my private Woodstock, begun by stepping through a traditional suburban doorway into a world no less wondrous than Alice found through the looking glass. The house was basic but had the necessities: piano, stereo, and not "jined on," as many St. John's rows of houses are, so there was no one to disturb in this parent-and-landlord-free zone. What was it about those years that furnace filters didn't need changing, and nothing ever broke? Or was it all broken and never fixed? I ran that house for five years and didn't own a hammer. (My husband has seven.) What about laundry and groceries, which later in life move from chore to ritual? "Thursday is our grocery night," one of those couples who look alike will say. It was a revelation to later learn that vacuum cleaners have bags that must be changed. Was there garbage day back then?

I get nervous now driving around St. John's when I see front-end loaders and diggers everywhere. In the search for incriminating oil tanks and archaeological remains, the whole town is being unearthed. What lies in the backyard of Poplar Avenue? Probably five years of dirty laundry and unwashed dishes. Before parties, we would stash the dishes in the oven; the trick was to remember to remove them next day before turning it on.

Things were fluid. No one got too exercised about anything. There were layers within layer of lives being lived. A friend asked me to store his cousin's motorcycle in the garage for a month. Sure, I said, and learned later that the carburetor and gas tank served as a cellar for his marijuana crop; his regular visits to check the bike should have tipped me off. (Another friend had a more clever solution. He worked for a public gardens and grew his own under the naïve but admiring eye of the deputy minister.) One day I opened the door to a guy I knew only slightly; he'd been at a party at the house the week before. He'd just spent the weekend in St. Pierre.

"Quick, your bathroom," he said, shoving me aside. I thought the ferry had upset him, but surely the four-hour drive from Grand Bank would have settled him down. I followed him up to the bathroom to find him standing over the toilet bowl. I watched as forty ounces of Courvosier gurgled its way into the wasteland.

"There was a roadblock on Kenmount Road," he said. "I thought they had me." He'd smuggled the prize booze successfully but the sight of a police uniform had triggered his paranoia.

At parties people we'd never seen before would wander in. One night a tall dark-haired Cher-type stranger, dressed in black except for a red plaid tam-o'-shanter, pushed her way through to me in the kitchen.

"Is there a *bed* in this place?" Her accent suggested a metropolitan background.

I nodded and before I had a chance to say it was *my* bed, she turned to the hapless fellow she was dragging behind her and said, "I gotta show this guy a thing or two."

It was a mystery to me what shy Ian, who hung out in a corner silent and stoned at all our parties, could possibly have done to antagonize or even tempt her, but off they went. (They're still together.)

Twice, in the middle of the night, I received phone calls from parents who accused me of harbouring their teenage kids. Both times I was asleep, alone, in my bed, having done nothing more dramatic the evening before than listen to a Mahler symphony. But the house had a reputation, only partly grounded in reality.

It was a pretty street in a sedate neighbourhood in what we called "the housing," as the area had been constructed after the Second World War by the Newfoundland Housing Corporation. All the streets were named for trees. Because the land was leasehold, there were some regulations; hedges, not fences, were the only border permitted in front, but no one had thought to place restrictions on exterior colours. I painted the house vermilion, so brilliant a red you could hide a fire engine in the driveway. The neighbours were unhappy, especially the guy who, before whipper-snippers were invented, used to kneel on the sidewalk outside his hedge and clip unruly blades of grass with manicure scissors. He was out of town during the change-over. On his first day back, he walked across the street like a tin man in need of oil, stiff with rage. "Easier for Santa to find," I said. I marvelled at his control – he really wanted to flatten me.

The paint job had been a collective project, various friends taking a shift, even an unsuspecting suitor. One day I was on top of the extension ladder stretching to reach the eave, the backs of my legs stinging, when a cheerful voice called out. I couldn't look down because I'm afraid of heights, but I was sure I heard the words "Starboard Quarter," a fancy seafood restaurant on Water Street. Dining out was my weakness and invitations were scarce, so I scrambled down to find a well-dressed young fellow with a dozen roses in his arms. I wasn't sophisticated, but at least I wasn't foolish enough to say, who are *they* for?

"I'll be just a minute," I said, passing him the paint brush. I went inside to change and put the flowers in water, then waited in my bedroom, reading, just long enough for him to finish the high parts.

One weekend I decided to remove the life of the house even more from the neighbourhood. Friends helped. We put fence posts in the ground and banged up a bunch of two-by-four and one-by-five boards. Perfect: an eight-foot-high fence, vermillion on our side, naturelle on the neighbour's. That guy also happened to be away while the home improvements took place. I don't think I was calculating; these were merely coincidences.

Poplar Avenue was modest, but it was mine (I'd inherited a small sum of money) and there were no rules. It was the era when the chair went out of fashion, for you'd no more walk into someone's house and sit in a chair than you'd perch on the mantle or the TV. We listened to the music of Emerson, Lake and Palmer, The Beatles, Jethro Tull (cringe) and Tubular Bells (double cringe), lying around on an orange shag rug, a rug with a life of its own. A visiting piano player once said it was the only house in the world where, in February, with boots covered in snow, salt, sand and slush, you could walk into the living room, sit at the keyboard and start playing before you took off your boots. One Sunday morning we were cleaning up from a party the previous night. Just as we thought we were done, my housemate, Maddy Williams, saw an old boot on the orange rug, sticking out from behind the piano. She yanked, and almost tore a muscle from the unexpected resistance: attached to the boot was one of her colleagues – a local actor known to drink – passed out cold junk. We had a small room off the living room that was lit only by black light. The walls were covered with the requisite black velvet posters that lit up in the dark, images so wild they made Salvador Dali look like Norman Rockwell. Cool. Hard rock – Pink Floyd, The Stones, The Who – was fun, zany, loud, and assured me I was definitely not living at home. It was recreation, entertainment, mood-enhancement; it created atmosphere and lent backdrop. I could "get off" on it, but I never once thought of it as music.

I remember countless nights of sitting around with some guy who'd scrutinize every word and image on the cover of a record jacket and on the liner notes, seeking secondary meanings, universal truths. Then he'd spin the record, up the volume and look at me with great urgency, saying, "Listen to that. D'you hear that?" But I never could.

In Mahler's *First Symphony*, I could isolate the lonesome pluck of the double bass at the end of the third movement, the funeral march. I could hear the short flourish of a three-note motif tossed off by the piccolo in the thickly orchestrated score of "The Moldau" from Smetna's *Ma Vlast*, but in the layers and layers of guitars and drums, synthesizers, electric this and switched-on that, I couldn't hear a damn thing. I *could* hear with exhilaration and anticipation

On Poplar Avenue with Kate Cooper. (Photo by John Doyle)

an incipient waltz in Richard Strauss' *Der Rosenkavalier*, the hint growing and growing as we waited breathless and, yes! the music blossoms and we are swept up in the full glory of a Viennese waltz, a waltz skewed and twisted, arriving at our ears as if through an aural convex mirror. I could hear all that. In the Berg violin concerto I could hear the hint of a Bach chorale as it begins to emerge, as if through fog, in the slow movement. But when it came to Pink Floyd or The Cream with their myriad layers of loud sounds, I was stone deaf.

They say women regularly tell guys one lie. I, too, am guilty of repeating one lie over and over to a long line of guys: yeah, wow, fabulous, ummm, more, please! But my fake enthusiasm, I hasten to add, was always in connection to music. The only record jackets that grabbed my attention were Janis Joplin's. I would stare, struck dumb at the photos of Janis, filled with envy and awe, wondering, How do you get to *be* like that? Where's her mother in all this?

I remember the sensation of listening to a live band play "Hey Jude" so loud you couldn't hear the music, you could only feel it. Music at that volume obliterates thought and dulls the surroundings, so all that's left is numbness. One night of the week I could play my flute searching for the subtleties and nuances that would make a Haydn phrase elegant. I could slave with my chamber music companions working through the transparent score of a Mozart flute quartet, breathing with them, thinking with them, trying to create perfect musical lines. Two nights later I could lie on the floor of the Thompson Student Centre at Memorial University in a haze of smoke, drifting, drifting, as the music pounded. No, it was more than pounding. It was enveloping me as if there was nothing in the world but that moment – that moment when you are inside the sound. This was beyond listening – it was immersion, and it was wonderful but, for me, it had nothing to do with music.

But my ears were open to the wonder that is Bach's *B Minor Mass*. With a friend who was a classical musician, I fell in love with the symphonies of Mahler, following along with the scores, marvelling at this genius of orchestration. We gave ourselves up to the tone poems of Richard Strauss, letting our imaginations be led around his huge aural canvass. On would go *Til Eulenspiegel* (The Merry Pranks of Til) and we were transfixed from that delicate opening moment with the violins. A handful of notes later the horns present themselves abruptly. The tympani aid and abet the fierce trombones and we're off – look out! – swept into the world of Til. We would listen breathless, tender violin motifs followed by bursts of terrifying brass, a musical roller-coaster ride. Threatening horns and trombones, insistent piccolo, they would mix together and tease us with a sleazy mocking sound. And Schubert: he had our souls as we wept our way through his *Winterreise* song cycle, the simple piano chords and melody scarcely preparing us for the sorrowing baritone who will take us on this winter journey: *A stranger I arrived here, a stranger I go hence.*

The eclecticism of those years! We were captured intellectually by Bach, imaginatively by opera, emotionally by Chopin and Brahms. I played two nights a week in a community orchestra and played for local productions of Broadway musicals. Some shows, such as *Fiddler on the Roof,* were tiresome; it was a drag to haul myself out the door every night for the weary descent into the pit. But when we played Gilbert and Sullivan's *The Mikado,* we knew it off by heart by week's end and could stand around the piano and sing the entire thing, including the localized jokes worked in to correspond with the changing political scene in Newfoundland. We would have informal chamber music nights, imitating the older players in town who, on occasion, would ask one of us to join their traditional evenings. All this around, and in, a house filled with Joan Baez, Bob Dylan, the Beatles, The Who, Genesis.

Around this time we had the bad habit of tormenting mainlanders, a natural result of having been tormented ourselves once too often over accent, choice of words, general naivety. We had the notion, too, that everyone from away was from Mississauga. One day a friend asked if the next time we were having chamber music night, he could drop off a friend who was visiting. Sure, we said, and along he came, violin in tow. He was a bit of a prig, with a lot of dork mixed in, the kind of guy who'd say "holy moly" where the rest of us would say "holy f . . . " We played a bunch of music and invited him back for a second night.

Before he came, we put on a record of a Mozart flute quartet played by Jean-Pierre Rampal and other outstanding artists. We recorded this onto a Sony cassette recorder, not using patch cords for a direct recording, but using a mike that picked up the living room ambiance and whatever we wanted to add: coughs, sneezes, turning pages, throat clearings. Then we hid the recording gear. When Mississauga Kurt arrived, we began to work on the movement we'd recorded earlier. After an hour or so someone suggested we record ourselves, just for fun. We made a pretense of finding the cassette recorder, set up the mike on top of a chair, and proceeded to play; we sneezed, coughed and turned pages clumsily at appropriate moments. When we finished, the cellist rewound the tape, going all the way back to the Rampal version. We sat and listened to "ourselves."

"Holy moly," said Kurt.

"Holy f . . . ," we responded.

"That's *us*? I had no idea . . . I can't believe I sound so good," but clearly he did believe and an hour later, after a cup of tea, we sent him on his way, generously allowing him to take the cassette home to play for friends.

"You're shockin', Marj, that's a sin for you," the cellist said before the door even closed, her upper teeth set down over her lower lip in the universal convent school expression for guilt and shame.

"Even's up the score," I said, reminding her of past grievances that had worked the other way.

I had never listened to the radio and didn't know the Top 40. In my early teens when I might have gotten the habit of radio listening, pop music was mixed up with wearing make-up and chasing boys. (I was with the good girls, practising flute and clarinet duets for the music festival.) The contemporary music I got to know later came from recordings bought, borrowed or traded with friends or older siblings. This was the era of the Saturday afternoon trek to Fred's Records on Duckworth Street, a sacred pilgrimage in an unhurried, savoured corner of the week: endless browsing, the hard moment of choice, the anticipatory walk home, cheerfully swinging the bag. On Poplar Avenue a new record came in like a long-awaited house guest. And there was time to listen, and listen, and listen again.

What are you doing Saturday afternoon?

I'm listening to a new record.

It was hard work. This was in the old days with maybe six songs on a side, fifteen minutes of listening before you'd have to rouse yourself and flip over the vinyl. Someone looking for a particular song or movement hovered over the dizzying turntable and tried to bring the stylus to a safe landing in the right groove.

I had been twenty when I walked out of the family home and into my own space. Music came in with me, that great vast package of short notes and long ones, soft and loud, a hefty parcel bursting with blues riffs, four-bar phrases, soaring melodies, plaintive arias, snatches of string quartets, electric guitars, stand-up bass, the Wagner Ring Cycle, the Beatles' White Album, Carole King singing and Carole King covered, a Brahms piano concerto one afternoon, Janis's "Mercedes Benz" that night. It came in a bulky expansive sack squeezing its way through the small porch, as palpable as the fridge and stove. Music arrived, settled in, spilling into every corner of a house that refused to put up musical borders.

Poplar Avenue meant freedom and that sense – never to be captured again – of the limitlessness of time. It was the beginning of adult life where your decisions are your own, where you answer to no one. It was a life filled up with music, generously embraced. My feet were planted in the classical world, and around that all other music could fit. On Poplar Avenue an oboist could work his way through the Marcello sonata with me clunking along the accompaniment at the keyboard, and an hour later, while he whittled his reeds, I'd switch to a twelve-bar blues back-up of a soulful "Jack Was Every Inch A Sailor," sung as we thought (and hoped) Sonny Terry and Brownie McGhee would do it.

The Practice Room

*S*ee ya.

The padded door closes with a small thud. I stare around the cubicle, six feet by eight, and look at my watch. The second hand crawls like a dying snail: one, two, three. I nod off and wake as the minute is finishing. Fifty-nine more and I'm outta here. Fifty-nine slow ones *toute seule*, unless someone knocks. But no one will. Not like high school where a ring of conspirators might sneak in, smuggling chocolates, chips and wads of gum. Around here they fight for this cell, reserve ahead; they *want* to practise scales, arpeggios, double tonguing, flutter tonguing and whatever else the guys who write those *vade-mecums* can think up. I look down at the instrument of torture: a long, cold, silver cylinder. I've spent far too much time with this bore, racing my fingers around it, gasping, breathing, pumping, wincing at that persistent hiss of runaway air.

I stare at the page, drag the flute to my lips and play. My God, it's ugly.

I'd practise, I honestly would, if I had one of those headsets construction workers wear when they're drilling with a jack hammer. Or the gear they use at firing ranges to muffle gun shots. Thin, pinched notes peep their way through a sprawling mist of escaped air. Through the fog I hear an E flat. E flat is good. Long tones, then, beginning with E flat. I drift, and some time later am woken by my own snores.

Breathing exercises would be more productive, and silent. We're supposed to stack books on our diaphragm to strengthen the muscles, but if I brought books in here, I'd read. I lie on the cold floor, remove my hiking boots, place them on my stomach and watch four pounds of footwear rise and fall. Ten times.

2:12. I open the door to get a cross draught. Keeners everywhere, scrambling towards the *Guinness Book of Records*. Longest note ever held on a clarinet, highest note ever squeaked by a tenor, loudest note ever screamed by a soprano. Scales in thirds, scales in sixths, piano players on the move. Cellists' palsied bow arms perfecting pizzicato, spiccato and . . . risotto? No, but I wouldn't mind some risotto, I'm famished. Every which way I turn, my ear is assaulted with crescendos, decrescendos, wispy little pianissimos. I close the door.

The piano stands seductress, temptress, inviting me to idle around those keys. Maybe someone will drop by for a jam, or mock opera. Forget it, there's always a spy-suck loitering outside who'll run and report that *someone who's not really serious* is hogging a practice room. Outside the window sociologists and philosophers stroll by, sipping coffee, gesticulating wildly. Once a year they slide thin essays under a prof's door with a note saying it's late 'cause they had scarlet fever. There they are talking, laughing, lolling about, as if the place is one big playground, as if this is not an institute of higher learning, as if there's no one in here sweating over melodic minor scales, two octaves, ascending and descending. More cheerful students, gear packed, are headed off campus, and it's only 2:19. Back to their lazy afternoons at their cool pads with stops at Ben's Pub for a beer along the way.

Temptation comes to the door. I let her in. Let's jam, she says. Can't. People will hear us. But when she leaves, my fingers troll the keyboard, fishing for harmony lush enough for Johnny Mathis's smarmy love song "Misty." I play chords, no melody, so it sounds like I'm working on keyboard harmony. 2:28. If only there could only be a fire alarm, or a bomb scare. Or a bomb.

I blame Sister C. If she'd assigned me the bassoon, I swear my fingers would be up and down that instrument like a squirrel chasing nuts. Or the cello: I'd whip around the fretboard, furies unfurled. But she sized me up, then handed me that cold, harsh, metallic impostor. Liar. Cheat. Fraud. The duplicitous flute. So innocent, easy. Oh you play the *flute*, people will say. I love the flute. It's so . . . well, so . . . flutey. So sweet. Like birds. Like nature. Like angels. Like *shit*. Give me a trombone and I'd be sliding around like a seal on an ice pan. I'd be marching through River City with Professor Harold Hill; instead, like the pied piper of Hamelin, the only thing I'm good for is chasing a pack of rats out of town. If they'd handed me the oboe, I'd be up before dawn whittling reeds – blue twine on my Mozart, red for Strauss, green for Paddy's Day, purple for Lent. The music of Marcello! Cimarosa! I'd . . .

The theory is practice makes perfect but, frankly, I've seen no evidence of this. I've clocked in years here, but the high notes still sound as if they're being yanked out with rusty pliers.

Breathe. Support. Exhale. Control.

I did. I have. I do. I will.

Put more air into the bore.

Bore? You've got that right.

It's like blowing across the top of a bottle, they told us first day at music camp. Which led us to abandon the flutes and start a bottle band. More fun and less work.

2:31. I've made a balls of this hour. Next lesson is Thursday. The prof's a good guy; I hate to see him cranky. Practise – to keep those furrows off his brow.

I look longingly at my Handel, God-love-him-Handel with those sweet suites, but my teacher is a modernist. OK, I'll tackle the Chaminade but first a stroll along the corridor so my legs don't seize up. I open the door, and get smacked by a cacophony of notes ricocheting, bouncing, buzzing, as if I've stumbled into the united nations of bees. I trip over the devoted, waiting for rooms to free up, waiting for wimps like me to walk.

Inside, the flute's gone flat. Warm it up. I should shine it. I take out my chamois and lovingly polish the instrument. It is quite beautiful, really. I read once . . . Yuck, it's gooey in there. Needs a proper cleaning. I take the instrument apart, lay the head and foot joints carefully on the piano stool, the body in my lap. I thread my cloth through the eye of the cleaning rod and ram it through, joint by joint.

That old flannel rag. All I got when we broke up. Boy, I loved that shirt. Brown plaid with the little hint of blue and yellow running through, so soft like the inside of the sleeping bag that first time, on the fishing trip and he . . . I whip the cloth through the foot joint, reassemble the instrument, sit up and give myself a talking to. I've got twenty-five minutes to *get something done.*

I haven't written my name on my new music, and it could go astray. I'm the only flute major and likely it would be returned but, to be safe, I'd better sign everything.

A schedule falls out. I fill in my class slots for the semester. It looks confusing, everything squashed on that tiny square. I highlight and colour code: practice, classes, rehearsals. I draw red stars by rehearsals, and outline the practice times in black.

It's busy in here. All the little housekeeping chores. I close the window to keep the instrument warm. I'm just settling down to the Ernest Bloch – jeeze, I hate that piece – when I see a chunk of resin on the floor. It's not urgent. Still, maybe I should hand it in to the office or put a notice on the bulletin board. I tear a sheet out of my exercise book, make a large sign, and colour it red. I start to draw a piano to illustrate the location of the resin, but give up after the keyboard. (I colour in the black keys.)

I open the window. If I stand here until May, I will see snow melt. It'll be like time-lapse photography, where someone sets up a camera in front of a blueberry bush and the camera films the whole thing and one day you end up at a film festival and there it is: three months of growth in one hour and it is truly amazing to spend that much quality time with a blueberry bush and not even get a piece of pie. It's like that, an hour in a practice room – as if I'm watching a film of myself that started years ago and will never end.

2:40. *What am I doing in music school?* I see myself at age six, sitting at the keyboard pecking out "Putt-putt-putt-putt-putt-putt-putt, goes the old type-wriiii-ter," and witnessing a minor miracle – squiggles on the page revealed. Not a word spoken then of the coming years of exile, the long lonely banishment to practice rooms. Accompanying, chamber music, stage band – I'll take it. I even gag down *collegium musicum* with its pitiful Renaissance flutes, those wusses of the instrumental world. But practise? It was a habit I never formed. At home, I'd play by ear for hours, puzzling out a new piece. (That made me ill-prepared for lessons but terror kicked in, producing excellent sight-reading skills.) I wouldn't mind sight-reading right now, except I was smart enough not to bring in distractions. Gee, I'm starving. I've got a rehearsal after this, two more classes, orchestra tonight. The Thompson Student Centre is next door. If I don't grab this chance – maybe I can't concentrate because I'm out of steam. Steam! I could use a sauna. That's half what's wrong with me. My body is stiff from holding this thing; it's not heavy, but it's bloody awkward. I mean, even without the hassles of the flute – say it was a broom you were holding, standing for hours with raised arms crooked at the elbows and skewed to the right, just hanging there. It's *unnatural*.

If I had a recording of Rampal here, I'd let him drown me out, him with his perfect limpid, clear, sweet, pure sound, his little stacatto hiccups, his long flowing phrases, his sly tongue fluttering around the passages, one minute soaring tweety birds, the next a sound as rich as Deep Throat. But I don't.

Practising, Samuel Johnson said, concentrates the mind wonderfully. (He said hanging, but there are parallels.) It prompts reflection on eternity. Through my mother's childish eyes I see the mountain of sawdust from the mill near her school. Every thousand years, Father Mahon said, a bird carries away one peck. One millennium, one bird, one peck. When the pile is gone, kiddos, eternity begins*, so you'd better hope you're not in hell.* That's the thing about the practice room – it can lead to metaphysical moments, reflective reveries, moral rejuvenation, epiphanies . . . Epiphany! Yikes, I haven't got a thing done for Christmas . . . But, really, there are occasions when you might want to slow down time. The doctor gives you six months to live. If an hour here feels like a month, then a six-month life expectancy increases exponentially and – well, it's a wonder the terminally ill aren't queuing for time-shares on practice rooms.

2:45. Get the tricky passages up to speed. First, chop them up into small runs. No, first: perfect articulation of one note. On second thought, I should begin with memorization. If I practise the piece on the piano, I could memorize it faster. It helps to *see;*

once you put the flute to your lips, your fingers disappear. Ymmm, the Bloch sounds good on piano. Sure, I was told, get a seasoned, second-hand Haynes open-holed silver flute with B foot, but if I had a shiny new flute, let's face it, there's fifty years worth of spit, spittle, guck . . . Ugh. I'm not putting that piece of crap *near* my mouth. Irrelevant, anyway, now that I'm going to practise the flute on the piano.

This is more like it. Why didn't I think of this earlier? One hand piano playing is easy, just a simple melody humming along. At my next flute lesson, I'll ask to play my pieces on the piano. I'll say I'm recovering from a root canal.

Still, that mightn't fly, so I should work on my embouchure – that perfect shaping of the lips and their placement on the flute. 2:51. I fish out a small magnifying mirror and set it on top of the piano. I check the position of the instrument on my chin, study the formation of my lips on the mouth plate, and . . . you know, maybe it's time I dropped my boycott against make-up. At twenty-two you need it. Look at those lifeless lips. If I played trumpet, they'd thicken up. I angle the mirror so I can't see my hair. I could make something of sagging cheek bones – possibly. That's something useful I could do right now. I could make myself up, if I had some make-up. I could nip over to the bookstore – do they sell make-up? I could look. The flute's sliding around my chin 'cause I'm hot and sweaty. I need some friction, like road salt for the flute. A bag of chips would do nicely. They should have a canteen in here, or even one of those carts they wheel around the hospital wards. For that matter, if I was in hospital, I'd hardly be expected . . . Anyway, I'm wilted. Ear training is less arduous.

It's not easy to test yourself – no one to plunk out notes while you, back to the keyboard, identify them. I turn away from the piano, stretch my arm behind me, and hit a key. Too easy. I know where I'm standing in relation to middle C. I close my eyes, spin around a few times to confuse myself, then stop and test me again. This works. I keep doing it until I've spun so much I stumble, knock over the music stand which takes out the flute on its way down. Ohmygod. How much damage have I done? Not enough, it appears, as I pick it up and it toots just fine.

2:58. I raise the flute to my lips and focus. Imagine a perfect note. Get inside that *Inside Tennis* thing, taking a page from a book that instructs you to play sports with your mind. I play an F, a perfect F. Never before has F sounded so true – not too low, not too high, not squeaky, squawky or fuzzy with impurities. A perfect round (yet not clouded), pure (yet not vacuous) F. Not a eunuch of an F, not bloodless, but a rich full-bodied F like a . . . like a good Bordeaux – would *that* go down nicely, a good Bordeaux. I should make fondue this weekend. Not fondue bourguignon – too many sauces, but I could do cheese, I don't have the right pot but I could borrow it from . . .

2:59:12. The second hand drags toward the finish line. You can do a lot in forty-eight seconds, but the next guy likes to start promptly at 3:00. And I like knowing the rooms are used efficiently.

The Walrus and the Nun

It was an eclectic round of rehearsals in those years: orchestra, marching band, musicals, and Gilbert and Sullivan shows all clustered around the central activity of "goin' to university, b'y," except no one did. "Goin' to university" was a cover or alibi rather than a statement of fact, providing the indolent and the imaginative with richer lives than simply having a job. At Memorial University of Newfoundland (MUN) there were "students" on campus for years who had never taken a course. (I think one later became premier.) And of those who did sign up, some descended into the tunnels and were never seen again, or at least not for a good long time.

The tunnels were an underground system of campus walkways, like an early mall without the shops. Because they housed the student lockers, the tunnels were the first stop of the day, and they might be the last, too: if there was a stash of comfort food in your locker, say a nickel of grass, you might lose a week down in that concrete warren. By midday it was like an obstacle course, trying to negotiate the tunnels without tripping over the stiffs, bodies half propped up against the walls of lockers like stuffed straw "guys" on the streets of London leading up to Guy Fawkes Day. Saying you were "up to MUN" didn't necessarily mean you ever set foot on campus. "Up to MUN" was often a state of mind, meaning you were free and had yet to take on the shackles of a job.

So in this period of "goin' to MUN" there was ample opportunity to sit around the house feeding the stereo, stopping it only long enough to bang out the music ourselves at the keyboard. The canon was Bob Dylan, Joan Baez, Joni Mitchell, the Beatles, Janis Joplin. I *knew* these songs, or thought I did until a few years ago at a party when I realized I couldn't sing a single word. My nieces and nephews, of a generation to be enamoured with Phish, *they* know all the lyrics from the 1960s and '70s. Words connect the listener with the song, but I can't reproduce one word from the hundreds of songs I heard and sang and played, again and again. Yet it was the age of poetry, campus literary journals, coffee houses; everyone and her brothers braved the stage. (My brother John, Kate Cooper and I called ourselves Cheap Tea and Molasses, from a line in the fierce Newfoundland ballad of the 1860s, the "Anti-Confederation Song.") If at any moment you didn't have a sheaf of obtuse poems in your back pocket, you were shit, or at least uncool.

When I listen to Bob Dylan now, he is so agitated, so earnest, trying to get me to hear his message. There is a sense of immediacy and urgency: *You gotta serve somebody, I said you gotta SERVE somebody.* Yeah, I hear you now, man, but I didn't hear you then. I lay around the floor of the Thompson Student Centre listening to local bands do covers of you, I bopped, tapped, rolled to you, I appreciated you, I *loved* you, but I didn't hear a damn word you sang! Go figure. My head was lost in post-convent fog not yet dispersed. I was holding myself back from full participation in my life, the delayed entry some fallout from a childhood and youth of warily picking my way through the banshee chorus wailing: not allowed, not allowed, not allowed. A distance grew up between me and – everything.

I was afraid of the consequences of any move. I might go out with a guy who'd get drunk, poke me in the back of his car and get me pregnant, or get drunk, prop me in the front and accidentally drive us over a cliff. There was the possibility of divine retribution for missing Mass on Sunday: whatever you were doing when you weren't at church, you might be killed doing it. In the early days of skipping Sunday Mass, I'd just sit still on a chair in the living room. What could happen there? I had a friend who'd dress for church, tell her parents she was off to Mass, and then spend the hour driv-

Cheap Tea and Molasses "in rehearsal" on Poplar Avenue – with Kate Cooper and my brother John. (Photo by Bill Doyle)

ing around in her boyfriend's Jeep. I didn't admire her insouciance, I shook my head at her folly. There was the fear that my mother would figure out that the photos from the camping trip didn't show one tent for boys and one for girls, just the same tent from different angles. Fear my mother would find out I was on the pill, fear that I'd be the one in a million for whom the pill didn't work, fear the dime of hash I'd bought came from some seedy sadist in "Tronto" who'd cut it with heroin and I'd be hooked for life. The winds of caution swirling around me since birth had an unspoken tag: if you do, then . . . I wasn't able to disassociate myself from life completely because I wanted too badly to live it, but I could keep back a step or two, and watch.

Maybe, *maybe* that's why I was always the one around the action, not in it. The role of accompanist suited me well; while others sang passionately, I sat at the keyboard and vamped, chorded, tinkled, improvised. The words swirled around me but never quite made it all the way to my brain. Most people don't hum the songs they like – they belt out the lyrics, even if the words are corny or tell a tale that's been told a thousand times. Think of the great musical storytellers like Tom T. Hall. His style is detached, his tone dispassionate, as if he's been hired to come on in, sit down and sing this damn thing. Can he be the same species as those pop stars who, when they're performing, look as if they might pass a kidney stone, or let their rupturing appendix spill onto the stage floor? They clutch the microphone as if to drop it would be sudden death. I like a Tom T. no frills straight-up tale of an old farmer in hospital wondering who's going to feed his hogs. There's a story to follow when Tom T. Hall sings about sitting in a lonely Miami bar. He gains wisdom from the old man cleaning up the lounge: there ain't but three things in this world worth a solitary dime – old dogs, children and watermelon wine.

That's how I feel *now* about the lyrics of a good song, but back then I hadn't heard of Tom T. Hall; he arrived in the country package that came later. As for Joni Mitchell, Joan Baez, and other great balladeers, the words passed me by. I wasn't introspective. I was out of step with my generation – I didn't like all the sitting around *talking* about things. I was a sensualist and preferred the moment. As for love stories, all those beautiful and torturous ballads, well, I didn't get them because I didn't get *it*. Love was a remote country busy with kissing and sin. Love was part of girls hiking up their skirts and tarting themselves up with lipstick. Not me. I was over in the good girls' corner. Expressions of sexual love, even "wholesome" family values stuff, was unfamiliar. I was raised by a widowed mother; she grieved for my father, but if she longed for a new partner, I did not know. I was privy to many things that a mature child in an adult household is, but they were not to do with my mother's emotions or needs. I knew if we were going to sell property or have a dinner party for visiting missionary priests, but I didn't know if she wanted to dress up nice and go on dates, or if she missed or craved male company.

All those lyrics, and in my own language: good poetry, riveting stories, rebel songs, wild expressions of anger, angst, joy. My response? Blank. I can rev up my 1991 Honda Civic in St. John's and head for Port aux Basques with a stack of cassettes to pass the time. My companions will sing every line of every piece. I'm tapping, bopping, moving, grooving, smiling, remembering great times, loving that music. I could stop by the side of the road, set up a portable keyboard and play the lot of it, *but I can't sing a damn word*. So I listen, as if for the first time. There are reasons buddy (in a Dylan song) doesn't want to work on Maggie's Farm no more. The brother, for instance.

> He hands you a nickel, he hands you a dime,
> He asks you with a grin if you're having a good time,
> He fines you every time you slam the door.

I get it! I met Maggie's brother later in the workplace. Too bad I hadn't *heard* the lyrics before; I could have whistled the tune every time I saw him coming. I put on a CD now and listen *for the first time* to the lyrics of songs I "know" well, songs such as "I Pity the Poor Immigrant" or "I dreamed I saw St. Augustine." For me, Dylan and Joan Baez and Joni Mitchell might have started writing yesterday.

Lyrics started washing over me without meaning in early childhood when I was introduced to songs and music in the oral tradition. In school, we were forever memorizing texts before they had meaning: songs, parts of the mass (first in Latin, later in English), hymns, prayers, poems for choral speech. Consider my ear and brain encountering the text from this Lennon-McCartney song, "I Am the Walrus":

> I am he as you are he as you are me and we are all together.
> See how they run like pigs from a gun see how they fly,
> I'm crying.
> Sitting on a cornflake, waiting for the van to come,
> Corporation tee-shirt, stupid bloody Tuesday.
> Man, you been a naughty boy,
> you let your face grow long,
> I am the egg-man, they are the egg-men
> I am the walrus
> Goo goo g'joob . . .

It could have been any old night at Benediction, rhyming my way through the litany:

> Mirror of justice, seat of wisdom, cause of our joy, spiritual vessel
> Vessel of honour, singular vessel of devotion, mystical rose, tower of ivory
> House of gold, ark of the covenant, gate of heaven, morning star.
> Corporation tee shirt goo goo g'joob – oops!

Except for the fact that we didn't pass around joints during Benediction, it was all the same to me. I was well primed to sing heartily and gustily, not held back in the least by lack of comprehension. And my mornings, my *every* morning, in the era of the Latin mass began with rhymes and rhythms like this:

> *Patrem omnipotentem, factorem caeli et terrae,*
> *Visibilium omnium, et invisibilium . . .*
> *Filium Dei unigenitum. Et ex patre natum ante omnia saecula.*
> *Deum de Deo, lumen de lumine . . .*

Is it any wonder that I could repeat words and sounds without troubling myself with meaning?

Where are all those songs, prayers, hymns learned by rote? I picture in a remote corner in my brain a gap the size of a mouse hole. If you shine a light in there, you will see it – one phrase, half phrase, or mumbled word. Poke your finger in, pry around a little and haul it forward. The whole thing will come tumbling out, expanding like an inflatable blimp filling up with all the mumbo-jumbo of childhood: every rhyme from the school playground, every skipping song, every hymn and fragment of prayer that was wholly memorized, scarcely understood. It's all in there, just waiting to burst out, every string of words we learned by heart with little or no comprehension. And every now and then, there is a Proustian release triggered by an aural madeleine.

With John, under a shamrock, drifting far from Irish music. (Photo by Kate Cooper)

    This happened one day in graduate school, during a class in sixteenth-century English literature. We were studying John Bunyan's *The Pilgrim's Progress* when suddenly my spirit flew out the opened window of the Arts building, over old St. John's, and back into the music parlour of my convent school. Standing before me was not the laid-back English prof but the director of my school glee club, leading our earnest little voices. I could recall the melody perfectly and the words too, although I had never given them any thought before. The incomprehensible text, and this was also the case with litanies and Latin hymns, was appealing enough linguistically to stay with a child. (Such childish delight in the mysteries of language was brought home to me when my niece told me that when she was a little girl just learning to read, I'd sent her a letter from Barcelona. She managed to read the whole letter herself, but the part she treasured was the delightful "Spanish" flourish I had thrown in for her at the end of one sentence: "etc.")

There I was physically sitting in a lecture room with casual grad school classmates, but in memory I was standing in my school choir spouting meaningless words in the dreamy way children do when they're rhyming off memorized texts. My brain only now is unscrambling the lyrics, guided by the text (from Bunyan's *The Pilgrim's Progress*) before me.

> Hob goblin nor foul fiend can daunt his spirit,
> He knows he at the end will life inherit.
> There's no discouragement shall make him once relent
> His first avowed intent
> To be a pilgrim.

So *that's* what it was about, that charming musical meaningless string we sang at age ten or eleven. I have never heard the song since and – as I have only my memory, not the printed music – I do not know whose setting we were singing.

(This has nothing to do with music, but shows how childhood images, as well as lyrics and music, can lodge inside our brains. One day, more than twenty years away from the Catholicism of my childhood, I was walking down an aisle in a Canadian Tire store shortly before Christmas. I stopped, paralyzed, a few feet before a display on the back wall. I turned quickly from what was surely the crown of thorns. The images of my childhood Christ on the cross came flooding back: the blood, the piercing, prickly, hurtful thorns digging into Him, digging into us and us feeling the pain because He did it for *us*. I composed myself, shook off the sick feeling and walked back down the aisle, forcing myself to look at the object rationally. It was some sort of rustic wreath made with sticks rather than boughs, called I think, a vine wreath.)

I learned Newfoundland songs, too, long before I knew how to read. We gathered around the piano at home, singing from songbooks our father had published. The songbook, *Old-Time Songs of Newfoundland*, had full-page ads with illustrations opposite each song. If someone called out "Kelligrew's Soiree," I turned to the page with the picture of the man in jail. The ads were for patent medicines, ointments and toiletries; in this case, a man who was "a prisoner of Backache" could get relief from Dr. Chase's liver and kidney pills. If "The Old Polina" was announced, I'd head for the woman powdering her face. Some company like Warner-Lambert must have sponsored that page. "Star of Logy Bay"? Find the woman sneezing into her hanky; this was an ad for Beech-Nut cough drops. I heard the songs over and over, but not yet able to read or even recognize the relevance of a capital letter, I didn't have the benefit of knowing that some words were the names of a person or a place. Any given line in a Newfoundland song was a mystery to me, but I could *sing* it with the best of them, indifferent to the meaning, in love with the sound, in much the same way as a young child sings "supercalifragilisticexpialidocious." My text was, say, from "The Kelligrew's Soiree":

> OhiborrowedclunysbeaverasIsquaremyarstosail
> andiswallowtailfromhoganthatwasfoxyonthetail
> Billycoudahesoldworkingpantsandpatsynolansshoes
> andanoldwhitevestfromfogartytosportat – Kelligrews.

This last word – the name of a place in Newfoundland – was recognized and confidently belted out. Even learning to read doesn't necessarily make the tongue go easily around Newfoundland folk songs. I've seen sophisticated friends from away stare at the page, blink, mumble and try desperately to move along with a crowd of Newfoundlanders singing. It's a challenge, even when you *can* read the words:

> Oh, I borrowed Cluney's beaver, as I squared my yards
>   to sail;
> And a swallow-tail from Hogan that was foxy on the tail;
> Billy Cuddahie's old working pants and Patsy Nolan's
>   shoes,
> And an old white vest from Fogarty to sport at
>   Kelligrew's.

Many of our songs tell real stories, tales of disasters, accounts of what happened to whom, when and why; it's easy for the lyrics to confound someone who's unfamiliar with our history and way of life. Our hundreds of sealing songs recount actual trips, who was in which ship, how many seals were caught, what happened in storms. Here's keen reportage from "The Sealers' Song":

> The Block House Flag is up today to welcome home the stranger
> And Stewart's House is looking out for Barbour in the Ranger;
> But Job's are wishing Blandford first who never missed the patches,
> He struck them on the twenty-third and filled her to the hatches.

In Newfoundland it is the seal hunt, not the daffodil, that is the first harbinger of spring. There's a nip in the March air as the ice flows south, bringing its floating population of seals, and signs saying "Flippers For Sale" appear along the St. John's waterfront. Traditionally, for men, it was the eagerly awaited break in the long winter months, the release from their confinement to land since they'd hauled up their boats in late fall. There was excitement and hard work in the preparations: competition to get a berth on a good ship, and providing wood and such comforts as could be given for the family left behind. There was the leave-taking in an age of little communication; a woman bade her husband goodbye, hoping she'd have no hard news to relay on his return. Hoping he would return. The trek, then, to St. John's to board the vessel – a journey, depending on the sealer's home port, made up of train, horse and slide, Shank's mare (walking). Then the time at the ice squeezed into the hold of a cramped ship, the cold, the weariness. The pride, weeks later, to walk through the kitchen door with cash, to pass over fresh meat to a wife who'd stretched salt fish and potatoes as far as she could.

Our hundreds of sealing songs have become more valuable now that sealing has been pushed along that strange trajectory, from working-class pursuit of food and wages to marketing tool for animal rights activists. They've packaged Brigitte Bardot, a cuddly seal, and selected images of a working sealer and sold it to the world as barbarism, an easy cause to embrace. As with any marketing message, it's been simplified, and it travels the globe as easily as the tracts in a missionary's suitcase. Of all the peculiar targets for ideological energy – not a sporting event for English gentry, such as fox hunting, but working-class toil, on a remote island. My grandfather made sixty-three trips to the ice, going two and three times some years. I'm relieved he didn't live to see the humiliation of the Newfoundland sealer.

I rattled off verses of Newfoundland songs at a young age, but they were incomprehensible until I learned to read. The songs became clear, then, because I was brought up at a time when we *knew* our island country well. It saddens me that songs and ballads placed before high school students in Newfoundland today would have to be glossed. Almost every second word needs the kind of annotation usually associated with poems and plays from the sixteenth-century and earlier. I could rhyme off "The Old Polina," which later proved to be a colour commentary of a race of whaling ships "from Dundee to St. John's." I could sing of the sealing disaster in which the vessel the *Southern Cross* and its 170 men went to the ice and never returned. The song recounts and records the details of the voyage and concludes with its offering of a tender, naïve consolation for

> The brave lads on the *Southern Cross* out in the storm
>   that day,
> We trust they reach that heavenly land and rest with Him
>   on high,
> Where cares and sorrows are no more, but all is peace
>   and joy.

Would that we knew the author of the bitter Newfoundland ballad "Hard, Hard Times," so that we could erect a memorial to him or her! The ballad reflects the futility and injustice in a life lived tied to the truck system. The truck system was a traditional system of credit in Newfoundland in which fisherman "sold" their catch to a merchant not for cash but for credit in the merchant's shop; the price of goods in the shop was set by the merchant. The ballad describes cycles beginning in spring and finishing up in the fall, "and when it's all over they've nothing at all, and it's Hard, Hard Times."

> Then next comes the doctor, the worst of them all,
> Saying: "What is the matter with you all the fall?"
> He says he will cure you of all your disease;
> When the money he's got you can die if you please,
> And it's Hard, Hard Times.
>
> The best thing to do is to work with a will;
> For when 'tis all finished you're hauled on the hill;
> You're hauled on the hill and put down in the cold,
> And when 'tis all finished you're still in the hole,
> And it's Hard, Hard Times.

I listen now to the masterful songs of the Beatles and Bob Dylan. It's an easy leap to sing a Beatles song without giving thoughts to the words if you've spent a childhood learning songs in an oral tradition. I tell you the truth: today, March 18, 2003, for the first time, I borrow my brother's music book and seek out the words of a "familiar" song. I have heard recordings of this song countless times, I've heard bands cover it, I've played the piano for a crowd singing it dozens of times, but now *for the first time* I read:

> Lady Madonna, children at your feet,
> Wonder how you manage to make ends meet.
> Who finds the money when you pay the rent
> Did you think that money was heaven sent?
> Friday night arrives without a suitcase
> Sunday morning creeping like a nun
> Monday's child has learned to tie his shoelace
> See how they run.

At least it's got the nuns in there.

Here's another mumbled gem regularly rattled off in childhood:

> O fragrant lily of all holiness,
> Captivate our hearts with your heavenly perfume;
> Receive, O most sweet Mother, our humble supplications,
> And above all obtain for us that one day, happy with you,
> We may repeat before your throne
> That hymn which today is sung on earth around your altars:
> You are all beautiful, O Mary.
> O crystal fountain of . . .

There the turquoise ink fades on my thirty-eight-year-old choir scribbler, and memory lets me down. This wasn't a prayer, it was a song! When other kids were wailing Petula Clark's "Downtown," or the Monkees' "I'm a Believer," I was crooning about supplication and fragrant lilies of holiness. This was my music, hummed walking home, sung in the bath. Is it any wonder that, after years of learning lyrics by rote and singing them heartily, I didn't really need to *know* what I was singing? Any surprise there was no imperative driving me to figure out what someone was talking about?

Sometimes it's different. I go see the Men of the Deeps, the coal miners' choir from Cape Breton. The men dress in work clothes and wear the traditional miner's hat with the powerful front light. They are entertaining and musical and humorous, but there is no forgetting how they earn their living. I am riveted by their storytelling. In one song (by Leon Dubinsky), a lone miner steps forward and, with his co-workers backing him up, tells the too-familiar tale of a father introducing his young son to the mine:

> Billy, come with me, come with me my son,
> I'll make you a man past your years;
> In the mine where the muscle is made out of iron,
> In the mine where the boys turn to men,
> In the mine where the strength of your back is your pride,
> In the mine where you're older than ten.

The story is simple, stark and plainly told, the images vivid. There is restraint in the singing, but the depth of feeling is undeniable. His passion – perhaps it is pain – moves us.

> Billy, stay with me, stay with me my son,
> You can't break a poor mother's heart;
> In the mine where the sun never shines on the black,
> In the mine where the count is your size,
> In the mine where your brain is of no use at all,
> In the mine where my dear brother lies.
>
> Billy went with him, went with him at last,
> As his father and fathers before;
> In the mine he learned strength from the wisdom of life,
> In the mine he earned monies to wed,
> In the mine where the coal has no use for a man,
> In the mine where young Billy lies dead.

This is an extraordinary choir. (The idea of a workplace choir defeats me entirely, having worked at the CBC.) They travel, singing their stories of work: of pride in their work, of the hardship of it, of the darkness and death they live with. They bring an uncommon personal knowledge to their music. You can't avoid the words, you can't not hear and respond to what they are telling you.

Slowly, I'm getting the hang of this *word* thing. I *can* now stick a tape into the cassette player in my car and sail out the Trans-Canada, making a quartet where there used to be a trio: Dolly Parton, Emmylou Harris, Linda Ronstadt, and me. The four of us cruise along, gently considering Jimmie Rodgers' song "Hobo's Meditation." We celebrate the free life of the harmless hobo and casually ponder his fate in the hereafter.

> Will there be any freight trains in heaven?
> Any boxcars in which we might ride?
> Will there be any tough cops, or brakemen?
> Will they tell us that we cannot ride?
> Will the hobo chum with the rich man?
> Will we always have money to spare?
> Will they have respect for the hobo
> In the land that lies hidden up there?

Still, I must confess that words will never be necessary for me to connect with music, for it is the melody, the harmony, the musicality of the performer that will reach me. I don't need to know the texts of the German poetry used by the great lieder composers. An opera is enhanced if I know the story, but I don't need to. Listen to Marc Dubois' recording of the aria "Je Crois Entendre" from the Bizet opera *The Pearl Fishers*. I promise you, you do not need to know the plot of the opera or the text of the aria to be captivated. He sounds as if he is in love with the music – not with his voice, as is the way with some actors and broadcasters – but with the music. He is tender, he caresses each note. His performance implies a respect for every phrase. We sometimes say that something is "unbearably" beautiful; this strikes me as literally true here. Sometimes I have to walk away from this piece.

And what of the magnificent soprano Renée Fleming when she sings Antonin Dvorak's "Songs My Mother Taught Me"? True, you've got the mother word in there, but I'm thinking of the simplicity of the song, less than two and a half minutes long. I'm thinking of the melody, the lyrical orchestral accompaniment, the quality of Fleming's voice and her musicality. Joanne Kolomyjec's recording of Dvorak's "Song to the Moon" from the opera *Rusilka* reaches out in the same way, drawing us in, causing us to gasp not because of the text, but because of the beauty and emotive power of the human voice.

Yet I know that it is text, words, that can bring people to music. I had a friend who described herself as tone-deaf. She simply could not distinguish anything going on in a piece of music. What must that be like, to hear an aural blur when a piece by Bach or Beethoven is playing! Because she appreciated literature and art, she knew she was missing out; she felt frustrated and deprived. The passion of her life was poetry. How could I sit by knowing the rich song cycles of Schubert and Schumann were not part of her world? I handed her the liner notes from my recording of the Brahms *Alto Rhapsody,* with its vivid picture of that dark Byronic brooding hero. Who cannot feel for the tormented traveller, the wandering soul seeking his way?

This is Brahms' setting of a text from Goethe's *Harzreise im Winter*. The contralto soloist sings with the mournful horns, bassoons and violas in torment and anguish, telling of the lost soul in the wilderness who has "drunk hatred from the cup of love." Think of that. I pause, as the music takes longer to express the thought. She brings before us this man "first despised, now despising." The vocal range is vast; the singer roams around the score expressing the wanderer's pain. The music is punctuated now and then by startling, powerful, stressful chords until, with a quiet intense preparation, the lower strings slowly climb note by note. In one magical, mystical moment, the music changes profoundly. With that one chord, the angst and worry and tortured sense are gone. In their place comes a hymn-like chorale sung by a male choir, gently pleading:

> If there is in your Psalter, O Father of Love,
> a song that can reach his heart
> Then let him hear it;
> Shine down your light on the thousand fountains
> surrounding his thirsting soul in the desert.

As the soloist joins the choir, there is still a level of anxiety growing and ebbing, but underneath the intensity, a gentle pizzicato pulse from the lower strings gives a glimmer of hope, offers a hint of resolution. Ultimately, the tension gives way. We feel relief for the wanderer, for all wanderers, for ourselves. We take comfort, as the music leads to a prayerful conclusion, to that cadence whose two chords almost universally accompany the word "Amen." The strings and horns hang on, sustaining the harmony, reaffirming the consolation even after the voices have died away. I walked my friend through this piece again and again, until she walked in through the door to music.

The Holiness Crowd

I am ten years old, hurrying to school late for some forgotten reason. The convent square and schoolyard are unusually empty at this hour. It's a frosty November morning but as always the tall old-fashioned windows are pulled down from the top and raised from the bottom. Music spills into the cold air. I hear a piece we have been learning in choir. I know the notes and words by heart, but suddenly I stop. The song is changed and what I hear is like nothing I have heard before. The beauty of the voices paralyzes me. Something inside me stirs but I can't identify what I feel. It is beyond happy and sad, yet elements of each of these are there. I rush inside, hunt through the row of hooks in the vast corridor and find a place for my coat and boots. I open the heavy wooden door into the room where the altos rehearse, but now the whole choir is squeezed in. We are assembled! Instead of sopranos downstairs in the parlour and second altos over in the passageway, we are singing together. What I was hearing, for the first time in my conscious life, was four-part harmony.

I found my place in the first altos and began to sing my part, blending, watching, listening, hearing how the line I knew now made sense; our humble alto line, often unmelodious, had a place. Sometimes weaving a third below the melody, sometimes punching out long notes to help give harmonic foundation, I sang as I had never sung before. Banded together, we altos proudly held our

The Presentation Convent Glee Club, after a winning performance in the Kiwanis Music Festival, c. 1965, flanked by our director, Sister Olivette (left) and our accompanist, Sister Hilda. Taken in our school auditorium. (School photo)

own, but now our strand of notes and phrases belonged to something new. It was as if we'd been handed a gold thread and told to wander in and out and around the others, ducking, diving, disappearing and reappearing, while the sopranos surfed above us. A brilliant aural tapestry shaped around us as all four huddles of kids wove their lines. I did not know the names Brahms or Mendelssohn, Schubert or Bach. I didn't know the words *a capella*, but my world was changed forever.

We had begun in September practising in four separate groups, first and second sopranos, first and second altos. One girl in each section, someone who could play piano and read music well, banged out the music, line by line, note by note. My duty was to the first altos, making sure each girl knew her part by heart. Notes and text. "Glow-reee-ah-in-egg-shell-sees-daaaaay-oh," we chanted a *Gloria*, furiously keeping track of how many beats for each syllable. There was a rough and tumble casualness, an insouciance when we were behind closed doors "without the nun" learning our part. We skitted and carried on, indifferent to the magnificence we were brushing against. But once assembled, all one hundred of us, our souls were lifted from pedestrian pastimes and brought to a higher plane as a procession of gifts inched into our childish lives: Brahms' "How Lovely is Thy Dwelling Place" from *German Requiem,* Mendelssohn's "Lift Thine Eyes" from *Elijah*, Bach's *Thou Guide of Israel,* Schubert's *To Music,* Mozart's *Alleluia*. All that and the most esoteric music I've ever sung – Gregorian chant. How did it all come together so that one moment we were kids in the schoolyard playing red-rover-red-rover-send-Carolyn-over, and the next we were transported into the kingdom of high art? Between skipping and jacks, we began a steady diet of aesthetic experience.

It was in that moment of first hearing four-part harmony that the mix-up began: the complicated tangle of religion and music that haunted me for the next twenty years. Because in that transcendental moment when for the first time I was moved by art, my mind, my soul and my heart got confused. I didn't know what an aesthetic was. If I had been forced to choose a word to describe what I felt, I would have said holiness. The emotion was so close to what I knew in our noble Basilica, surrounded by iconography and breathing in incense and oils and candle wax: awe, sacredness, mystery and wonder, a feeling of otherness, of being removed from the every day. There was an evaporation of the here and now, the physical surroundings dissolving into irrelevancy. At the same time there was an elevation – or perhaps a moving aside – to another place, a place entered into first with the heart, then with the head. I found my way to the temple of art through the temple of religion.

At the time I began singing I was a convent girl, writing away for booklets about becoming a missionary nun, receiving Communion every day, whispering delicately in church if I had to speak at all. I followed the routines of the church like an old woman, making the stations of the cross, saying the rosary, going to Benediction with its glorious recitations of the litanies, and attending daily Mass. As was the way with old crones passing the church who wanted to make a visit, I would clip a tissue onto my head with a hairpin, obeying the church's edict that women not enter church bareheaded. Morning after morning I knelt at the cold marble altar rail, closed my eyes, extended my tongue and received the "Blessed Sacrament," the thin wafer about the weight of bond paper, made by the nuns in the adjoining convent. I remember the feel of the host on my tongue and the delicate mystical moment between receiving and swallowing, without my teeth touching it, as was the rule. I have never "tasted" wine with so sensitive a palette. I *remember* the taste and after-taste of Holy Communion.

When I rose from my knees, turned and headed back down the aisle, the feeling was the deepest I had ever experienced and it was tied to the absolute unwavering conviction that Our Lord was now within me – that, as in the Communion prayer, he had "come under my roof," that with this arrival "my soul [would] be healed." The sensation was spiritual, but it remained part of my life, long after I had lost every vestige of holiness, every belief. The feeling stayed but became tied to music, in particular sacred choral music. The power of association had something to do with it, for all the while I was walking up and down the aisle, I was hearing and singing simple but beautiful Latin hymns such as "*O Salutaris*" and "*Tantum Ergo*." They belonged to the church itself, that magnificent palace with its gold painted ceilings, ornate decorative mouldings, stained glass windows and statuary.

The Roman Catholic Basilica was a Newfoundland Taj Mahal with a resonating acoustic. Even silence was alive, palpable, potent – laden with tiny sounds about to break out and bounce around the rich vast chamber. Here, an old woman's whispered penance travels several pews ahead; the clasp of a handbag fires like a gun shot. Coughs and sneezes are epic. An old man's nose-blowing sends a worshipper running for cover. In the silence, the opening of the main door at the back of the church offers not a squeaky hinge, but a majestic swoosh; a squeal is ennobled. The music of our liturgy bounced around this glorious temple, filling it up with sanctity and reverence. Thirty years beyond my childhood, I was in the Basilica at a rehearsal one night when a young man came up the aisle carrying a Tim Horton's coffee and a doughnut. If he had galloped up the transept naked on horseback, he couldn't have shocked me more.

In high school, we had our own chapel and I – still surprisingly devout, several degrees at least removed from normal teenage pastimes – attended Mass every day. After I received Communion I would walk directly from the rails down to the organ where one of the nuns was playing the Communion hymn. I would slide onto the stool next to her from the left, and gently inch over as she slid off the stool on the right, thus allowing her to go to the rails. We would do this "hand-over" on a sustained chord on the electric organ without skipping a beat, literally; the congregation was never aware that the person who finished the hymn was not the one who'd begun it. This ritual, perfectly executed every day through my high school years, strikes me now as efficient, practical, beautiful, and bizarre. (As a devotee of detective fiction, I can't help but think of the possibilities this allows for in terms of alibi. If I ever manage to write a mystery story, keep a close eye on the organist.)

In those younger years, the church was the centre of my existence. My world was peopled with the holiness crowd: saints, the devil in all his guises, my guardian angel and a host of other angels, and the Holy Souls in Purgatory, desperate for my prayers. These were particularly precious because my father was among them, waiting for our prayers to lift him from Purgatory and gently ease him into Heaven. There were my patron saint, the Holy Family, Our Lady of Perpetual Help, the Infant of Prague, and all other representations and manifestations of Christ and the Virgin Mary busying around my head and heart. No wonder it was so lonesome when they left. It was like finding yourself abandoned after your family immigrated to a new country. I was lost, wandering out there in a new godless universe, and the trigger that could bring the package back, with a stab, was music.

Many years later, as a radio host, I had to return to the Roman Catholic Basilica of my childhood, that opulent art gallery of nineteenth-century Newfoundland, to host a live broadcast of Handel's *Messiah*. I was haunted by despair, completely out of place with the joy and hope that Christmas *Messiah*s bring. From where I was seated, I could see the upper gallery where my grade five class had sat, the front pews where my grade seven class had knelt, the shrines and side altars I had frequented "making visits" to get indulgences. I could see the dramatic bronze representations of the crucifixion and death of Christ – the fourteen stations of the cross I had coursed hundreds of times to fulfil obligations promised in spiritual bouquets, the abstract package of prayers and rituals presented as a "gift" by young girls to their mothers or favourite nuns. All of this had been associated with music. Now, in front of a radio microphone, I had to fight the hollow inside me. For years, I could go into a church if there was no music, and I could sing sacred choral works in a secular concert hall, but church and music was a deadly blend. It took years for the separation to be complete. You can't have a presence in your life for the first twenty years – something beautiful, deep and consoling – and give it up easily. The feeling that lingered inside me wasn't spiritual, it wasn't the last dregs of faith. It was grief. I spent the first years of my apostasy in mourning, because I had lost something irretrievable. Music served as a reminder, a symbol for "things past."

It is hard to explain this because now when I have to enter a church for a wedding or christening, I feel nothing; I won't say numb – numb is suggestive. With the exception of the Basilica of my youth, a church now is just a building, like any other. I look at the clergy dressed in absurd costumes, commanding attention, and I marvel that people give themselves over so easily to others, volunteering as captive listeners to whatever spiel the clergy wants to spout. (The worst I experienced was a priest – and we are told priests are celibate – using a young couple's wedding day to rant about marriage and divorce. We, the divorced, wanted to walk out, but how to do that without spoiling the day for the bride and groom?)

In a way, the Catholicism of my childhood offered everything children love. It contained mystery, ritual, ceremony, costumes, lighting candles, and magic potions like incense. If I wanted to give some little girls I know now a treat, it wouldn't be McDonald's or glow-bowling. I'd stage a High Mass from the 1950s. Let the kids dress up as priests and altar girls, let them light candles, and swish the incense thurible, and give them the mumbo-jumbo lines of a mystifying language. Because that was part of the lure: a secret unknown language.

From grade seven on, we studied Latin as an academic subject, but even earlier we were introduced to church Latin; we were taught to pronounce the parts of the Mass the congregation spoke aloud. Latin was memorized sound learned by rote and from repeated usage. I was brought up going to mass *every morning*, so the words of the *Gloria*, the *Credo*, the *Sanctus* and *Benedictus* were second nature to me. Later when I would come upon a Haydn Mass or the Fauré *Requiem*, there was comfort and warm memories, the sounds bringing me back to the best part of my childhood. When I encountered a *Stabat Mater* by Dvorak or Pergolesi, I heard familiar lines: *Stabat Mater dolorosa juxta crucem lacrimosa*. I know the gist of the stark scene crouched in the Latin text:

> At the cross her station keeping
> Stood the mournful mother weeping
> Close to Jesus to the last.
>
> Christ above in torment hangs
> She beneath beholds the pangs
> Of her dying, glorious Son.
>
> Is there one who would not weep
> 'Whelmed in miseries so deep
> Christ's dear mother to behold?
>
> Bruised, derided, cursed, defiled
> She beheld her tender child,
> All with bloody scourges rent.

The *Stabat Mater* text has been set by many composers, including Rossini whose setting moves from reverent to slightly crazy – the music is pure Rossini, reminiscent of his best comic opera self, while the text is so bleak. There are various settings, too, of the *Regina Coeli*, again familiar to me after a childhood of Benediction, Litanies, and Vespers. Franz Schubert has set this text more than once, each setting glorious:

> Queen of Heaven, rejoice to see, alleluia
> For he whom thou was made worthy to bear, alleluia
> Has risen as he said, alleluia.

There: the central tenet of Christianity – the resurrection – expressed with poetry and simplicity. Add the genius of Schubert and it becomes a work of art. No wonder it took me so long to untangle those two powerhouses!

I once had the shattering experience of watching those around me fall likes flies, one after another, into the clutches of a Christian fundamentalist cult. They cut themselves off from society. They began by throwing out the television: they unplugged it, carried it to the sidewalk and left it there. They discontinued subscriptions to the daily newspaper and household magazines. They wore headsets and lay in their beds at night listening to the mesmerizing rhetoric of their preacher. This cult (not their word) believes the seat of the Antichrist is Rome, that all Christian art including music is taboo. Everything associated with the intellect or with aestheticism is anathema. The American founder of the sect, claiming he was not materialistic, boasted he had only two possessions he cared about: his Bible and his gun. Everything is excluded: Christmas cribs, statues (false idols), stained glass windows, robes or vestments of any kind. This extreme right-wing sect points to the 1950s American TV sitcom *I Love Lucy* as the representation of the moral decline of the modern world. (In my bones I know this has at least something to do with a woman as star.)

Desperate to distance themselves from mainstream churches, the new followers rejected anything considered an adornment, anything fancy that might clutter up, or divert attention from, the unilateral interpretation, by this one man, of Biblical texts. Down with the rest of it. Yet when I have sung in the chorus of the powerful Mendelssohn oratorio *Elijah*, I stood there knowing there can be no more effective way of telling the story of Elijah and the prophets of Baal. When the cocky followers of Baal cry out for his help and don't get it, when their mild confusion at the lack of response turns to terror, I sit on the edge of my seat and sweat. I suffer horror, but also feel relief and joy as I listen to this story (in English). There is holiness, fear, anger in this tale. Can any preacher convey the power of this story, can any preacher *tell* the story as Mendelssohn does through his setting of the text?

Fundamentalists are not the only church goers who have made curious decisions about church music. Mainstream churches, too, have swept their traditional music out the door in the hope that if pop music was brought in, congregations would grow. I've never been convinced of this. With the exception of gospel and spirituals, most church music today is unmemorable. This reasoning was based on a fallacy anyway, for churches did not embrace contemporary music; they merely switched from one dated music to another. To pretend that the folk songs with guitars that are sung in church today are "contemporary" must seem laughable to the under forty set. In the 1960s, the Catholic church switched to the folk music of the day – and they have stayed there. If it were truly contemporary, we'd be hearing grunge, punk and rap in churches today. To bring into church music that the congregation can relate to as their "pop music," you'd have to have Frank Sinatra for the old folks, Bachman Turner Overdrive for the Baby Boomers and "alternative" artists for the teens. Churches are ignoring the power of music to stimulate deeply spiritual experience in favour of supposed accessibility. Art has been removed and replaced by insipid, unworthy, aural dishwater.

I'm not a missionary and I belong to no church, but I offer this recommendation to anyone trying to rouse sleeping souls. Find a recording of the Monteverdi Choir singing Schubert's setting of Psalm 23, "The Lord is my Shepherd," set for four-part female choir and piano. Go to a public place – Speakers' Corner in Hyde Park in London, Skydome in Toronto, or Churchill Square in St. John's. Bring a good stereo system and speakers; you'll probably need a small generator as well. (Better still, hire a choir!) The piece is sung in German, so you might want to pass out a leaflet with the text translated, but you needn't – the music will speak for itself. The mighty will fall, the arrogant will bow their heads, the greedy will empty their pockets, the villains will rid themselves of vice. Hardened hearts will melt, while old enmities will seem insignificant and slowly fade away. Resentment, anger, bitterness will be replaced by a notion that there is something more worthy of us all. For some, this will be religious belief and they will wander new into your congregation; others will climb an alternative path to a different god. No one will remain unchanged.

Most of the choral music I've sung has been sacred, which is not a reflection on me, but on choral repertoire. Historically, many composers wrote sacred music as gigs and paid assignments either directly for the church, or indirectly, through court or state. Others, even in the twentieth century, chose sacred texts for their choral masterpieces, turning again and again to the Mass and the Requiem Mass, psalms, and prayers such as the "*Ave Maria*" and the "*Ave Verum.*" The genre is huge. If you stumble onto it, you have a lifetime of music with a long shelf-life. And you don't have to believe a thing. It is rich, even for the skeptic.

I was lucky: that marvel unfolded for me at a young age. It was a gift, an entryway into a magnificent country of beauty and hope and promise. It was a way for a child to be part of making high art. To stand in a four-part harmony choir and sing Bach was to be passed a paintbrush and offered to help touch up spots of the ceiling of the Sistine Chapel. It was as if Michaelangelo had passed me a child's tool set and said, Hey, kid, you can help chip at David's toe, and here's a chamois to smooth it all off when we're done. To sing the choral repertoire we sang was to be lifted into a world children rarely get to enter, but it had another function, too.

I was a skittish kid; the annual complaint from a long line of teachers to my mother concerned my "deportment." I was idle, always seeking the good time lurking inside the rigid day. I wrote notes, fooled around and talked, a champion at clocking in the maximum number of whispered conversations that can be squeezed into a school day. I had a fine time of it, in school. I was sociable, outgoing and happy. But underneath, I was worried, worried the way a kid alone with a widowed mother is. Our family life had changed radically from a house full of brothers to the still house of a widow and child. Kids share secrets, but I never shared. I was bottled up, tight inside. I kept my emotions well stowed. But I tumbled gratefully into the warm hideaway of my childhood – choir.

Mr. Foggin's Fellows Come To Town

My childhood was filled up with the regular pursuits. Outdoors the schoolyard was a girlish arena of skipping (ones-and-in-bys, twos-and-in-bys, Dutch, and French), in-and-out-the-windows, hopscotch, kick-the-stone, boys-boys, and red-rover-red-rover. Indoors there were marbles and a never-ending game of jacks with the subsidiary rounds and challenges: memory is dim but, sweep the floor? in the basket? over the hatch? up your hole? (No, surely not.) Above, beyond, and in between was music. The organizing force was Trinity College, a British system of external examinations in which children throughout the colonies could be graded and attain levels in choral singing, choral speech, piano and most memorable of all, theory.

Trinity College differed in two ways from everything else we did: it was secular, unrelated to our church-ridden world, and it was outside the command of the nuns. In a gender flip, we were brought up in a universe run by women, educated women with authority. The only men in our school were servants of the nuns – janitors and drivers. Our grey stone building was attached to the motherhouse; a passageway led from there to the Basilica, and the Basilica was joined on the other side to the bishop's residence, known as The Palace. We were part of a magnificent, sprawling granite kingdom dating to the mid-nineteenth century. But in the territory of Trinity College, the nuns were part of a larger game, and they observed the rigid strictures in a way that made our everyday slavish attention to all things religious and scholastic seem flighty.

Everything about Trinity College had mystery and lore. In addition to the number assigned to each grade level, there was a parallel terminology: First Steps, Preparatory, Advanced Preparatory, Intermediate, and Higher Local. (What did *that* mean?) But it was hard to confound us with curious nomenclature, we who were brought up with a vocabulary that included mortification, extreme unction, holy orders, transubstantiation, novice, postulants, breviary, missals. What word could seem odd to us who memorized these lines from the Litany of the Sacred Heart: "tabernacle of the Most High, burning furnace of charity, abode of justice and love, abyss of all virtues, loaded down with opprobrium, bruised for our offenses, pierced with a lance, source of all consolation." It would take more than *andante con moto* or *piu mosso* to get a rise out of us.

Of theory itself, there was the appeal of getting inside a logical, complete and independent system of knowledge, of knowing strict rules, of working things out. Some people get this elation from mathematics, but the only joy I felt during algebra or geometry class was when a note came to the door saying I was wanted for an extra orchestra practice. With theory, there were the laws of harmony, and the satisfaction of seeing why the notes of a chord fit together as they did; of knowing how to arrive at this key from that key, understanding which notes fell within a particular key and which were outsiders (accidentals). There was an excitement in knowing how to write out the harmony implied by a few given numbers in "figured bass," in knowing how to construct a major or minor scale. Within the minor scales, there were two possibilities, harmonic and melodic, each with its own patterns to be memorized and, with luck, understood. There was the delicious appeal of the rich vocabulary, like cadences – two successive chords used at the ending of a piece or a phrase. The typical "Amen," for example, is called a plagal cadence, but there are also the perfect cadence, the imperfect, the phrygian and the interrupted cadence.

Along with cadences, there was the wild and wonderful vocabulary of notation. Notes which since have gone the dull American route of mathematical description – quarter notes, eighths, sixteenths – were colourful in our Trinity College world. They were quavers (eighth-notes), semiquavers (sixteenth-notes), demisemiquavers and, but of course, hemidemisemiquavers. Quarter notes were crotchets, and half notes minims. Once or twice a year we encountered the longest note of all – the whole note, curiously known as the "breve." And I haven't come yet to the Italian vocabulary used in music: allargando, fortissimo, prestissimo, allegro molto, decrescendo poco a poco, tierce de picardie. Also diminished by bland Americanization, which means Canada adopted it too, are the now prosaic "grace notes," or ornaments. To us, these were acciaccatura, appoggiatura, and mordents. No wonder the words in our spellers seemed easy. Standing alongside the wall of the music parlour, we were quizzed and drilled on these words, the same as at a spelling bee, luxuriating in the fanciful linguistic delight of such magical words. The intrigue didn't lie only in the spelling or pronunciation of these words; the whole package was like being part of a secret club. I'm reading now from scribbled childish notes in my manuscript book of perhaps the mid-1960s:

> The appoggiatura takes:
> a) one-half of the value of a note [divisable] by two (dotted or otherwise)
> b) two-thirds of a long note [divisable] by three (dotted crotchet or more)
> c) one-third of short note [divisable] by three (dotted quaver or less)

And in case anyone asks:

> The acciaccatura in Andante or faster, write as demi-semiquaver. Slower than Andante, write as hemi-demisemiquaver.

Such were the mystery and intrigue of Trinity College. If you're stuck at a cocktail party, it might stand you in good stead.

The theory examination was held on the first Saturday morning in December, conflicting every year with the Santa Claus Parade. We were used to spending Saturday mornings at school for glee club, but there was still a sneaking pleasure being in the building "after hours," as if we had been let in on a secret. We didn't have to wear our weekday uniforms, but we couldn't dress down. Jeans didn't exist then, except perhaps as dungarees worn by boys in summer or farmers in books. We wore skirts and dresses as if we were going to perform, although all we were going to do was sit an exam in a classroom.

There have been many examinations in my life throughout school, university, music school, grad school. Often these were held in gymnasiums with rows and rows of desks, rows so long you needed an usher to find a place. Pacing vigilantes practised the kind of policing that makes the innocent feel guilty. I was afraid to raise my head for a second for fear of being caught cheating, although I have never cheated. And I had to relearn sneezing, reining in my dramatic convulsions lest gestapo eyes interpret my full body writhing as a sneaky peek at my neighbour. But no exam setting could compare to the solemnity of the Trinity College theory exams, which began when we were as young as eight.

Once a year, on that examination day, the senior classroom at Presentation Convent was transformed to a sacred place, a temple to Trinity College. The room had neat rows of old-fashioned desks fastened to the floor; the desks had tops that opened to allow for storage of books and scribblers, an indentation for pens and pencils, and a hole for an inkwell. At the front of the room was the rostrum that held the teacher's desk. There were small side altars with statues of the Infant of Prague, the Sacred Heart, Our Blessed Lady. On Trinity College day, it was as if the room had been shrunk, pushed through a C.S. Lewis hole in the back wall and replaced by a brand new chamber, the atmosphere was so altered. Adding to the unfamiliarity was the presence of two boys, thought to be Protestants studying privately with some retired nun. On our diplomas, which arrived months later, this humble classroom appeared as the "Newfoundland Centre."

We waited outside the locked room until minutes before the set examination time. We entered and found our assigned places. We were used to a "no talking" dictum, but this really was no talking. What would the punishment have been if we had? Disqualified, I suppose, but as with most children's punishments, it is not the punishment that carries weight; the currency lies in what it conjures up in the child's mind. Manuscript paper for our rough work was lying on our desks when we arrived. When everything was settled, a nun would arrive at the door, pass in a package to the attending sister who, standing on the rostrum in front of us, broke the seal on a large manila envelope. The papers were passed out in silence. What I cannot remember is, did we pray? Before all our classes in school we said a prayer, so not to do so would seem odd. On the other hand, we were in secular territory and there may have been rules forbidding this. If I could track down those Protestant boys, likely they'd remember.

The examination papers were long, a single sheet printed on both sides. Some questions required naming chords, or analyzing short passages of music. In these cases, the staves, clefs and music appeared on the sheet, printed with the authority of a publication, awaiting our answers. These were not papers that had been "stenciled off" with a blotchy purple ink, as school tests often were. These were printed documents, formal and intimidating, not the products of Gestetner or Xerox. We could take nothing into the examination room except a cartridge pen, a pencil for rough work, and a razor blade to correct errors. Erasers were forbidden. We tried hard not to make a mistake, and using rough work helped, but even when copying from rough work it's easy to err. If so, we had to get the ink off with the razor blade and write in the correction. (Try doing it, in an idle moment, without putting a hole in the paper.)

The sophistication of the examination questions depended on the level. In higher grades, there were transposition, harmonic analysis and modulation (key changes), intervals and figuring, and harmony. My diploma for First Steps, taken when I was in grade two, reads:

> Marjorie Doyle, Pupil of Presentation Convent, Cathedral Square duly passed in Pitch, Notes and Rests, Time, Keys and Scales with honours at the Local Examination held at the Newfoundland Centre in December 1961.

The first missed Santy parade.

After the examination, we had to leave our rough work on our desks but it was returned to us later. To add to the suspense, it was weeks, perhaps months, before the results came back.

"Trinity College's in," a girl-spy would rush to tell you in the bathroom. The bathroom, a big room with three or four cubicles and a strong smell of Jeye's Fluid and Dustbane, was like a post office in an old outport – a centre for news and gossip.

"Ohmygodbetifailed," was the usual reply, a girl smacking her forehead in horror at the thought of what might come later that day.

The theory exam, theory classes and all our music brought us to school early, kept us late – after dark, for most of the school year – and returned us there on weekends. Our school during off-hours had its own curious ambiance. Emptied of the busy but orderly population, the majestic staircases and polished wooden bannisters seemed more stately, the corridors, with their dark hardwood floors, immense. Vacant classrooms gave off an eerie feeling, as if their quotidian life had been frozen mid-moment before the rooms and corridors emptied, spilling hordes of little girls out into the daylight. The classroom doors were wide-open to the hollow corridors. There was the implied life: the smell of apple core and pencil shavings mixing together in an unemptied wastebasket. Spelling tests and progress charts hung on the walls and, according to the liturgical season, there were May altars, June altars or the Christmas Crib – replaced in contemporary classrooms, no doubt, by pin-ups of The Backstreet Boys and banners about Thanksgiving. (Thanksgiving was unknown in Newfoundland during my childhood, the concept imported and delivered unto us later. The unfamiliar two-part word showed up in our speller in grade four or five: Thanksgiving Day, two words, and don't forget the capital letters. But what *was* it?)

And passing by the classrooms, looking through the opened doors, there'd be other remnants of the weekday life, like ragged-looking gaiter bags, stitched together by harried distracted mothers. We kept our winter boots in these small drawstring sacks, hanging them on our coat hooks in the cloakroom at the back of the classroom. The gaiter bags, made from odds and ends of curtains and cloths from around the house, turned an empty cloakroom into a Jackson Pollock gallery. There were tell-tale signs of a classroom vacated quickly, such as a blackboard not rubbed off. We never used the word "erase." It was always Str (short for Sister and pronounced stir), can I rub off the board? Answer: *May* you rub off the board? Yes, you may. How hungry was our childhood that to "rub off the board" was a cherished task? We were not tearing off after school to waiting minivans that would transport us to dance class or swimming parties or Tubby Tubular climbing gyms. We hung around, looking for chores that would delay our departure. And we were all day long finding excuses to open and close the windows – eight feet high or more, raised from the bottom, lowered from the top with a ten-foot pole. It was an unwieldy pole and heavy. Sometimes a girl would be five minutes staring up, weaving, trying to navigate the hook into the hole at the top of the window, like fishing upside down.

There were other coveted duties, the best of which was "to go 'round with a note." In one part of our school there was no PA system and, as there were often announcements, a messenger was essential. I always wanted to be the one chosen, out of restlessness, or a desire to get out into the corridors to find another girl to talk to. I had a vague yearning, too, to be a dutiful lieutenant – I often felt tempted to salute and bow when I would knock on a classroom door and be greeted by a girl inside. (There was competition every year to get the first desk in the row nearest the door so you could be the one to answer knocks.) Sometimes knocks brought the principal, but usually it was a girl with a note.

The note, which would be passed to the teacher and then read aloud or not accordingly, might be "Jenny Foley is to go to her piano lesson at 2:00 today, not 2:30." The trouble with that kind of note was the short shelf-life – it went to only one classroom. The best notes were the generics which all classes had to hear. In my old school, now a multi-million dollar condo property in downtown St. John's – a former lieutenant-governor lives in my grade three classroom – we were spread over four floors. The real estate flyer could tell you how much linear territory and cubic space we covered when doing a note; the realtor could have used me as poster girl when flogging these units, so well do I know the territory. A note with high currency might be: "Sister Mary St. John of God would like all the money for the Monsefu mission collected by tomorrow afternoon." Or it might be a change in time or cancellation of a glee club rehearsal.

It was glee club that brought us into another dimension of the Trinity College world. Theory was fall work; in the spring we concentrated on our "practical," when the Trinity College examiners "came out" from England to hear and evaluate us. These annual spring visits included piano exams. These took place in the grand parlour of the convent in order to allow us to use the best piano on the premises. They featured a curious tableau: child at the keyboard, nervous; foreigner at a far-away desk, scribbling; nun outside the door, listening. The value of a pass in the autumn theory exam was its use in the practical exams. When it came to the mysterious *Viva Voce*, the word "exempt" was marked on our reports, and we were given full marks for that section. The practical exam consisted of solos, studies, scales and exercises, ears tests and sight reading. The drawing room was huge and majestic. I'd like to see a photo gallery now of the examiners who were "sent out" each year. In my memory they were always the same: tall, gaunt, remote and cross. During the course of the exam, which probably lasted twenty to thirty minutes, depending on the grade level, the examiner spoke only a few words, just enough to request which scales and arpeggios he'd like to hear.

"I should like to hear F minor, please."

Think! key signature, quick, but not so quick you don't get it right.

"Very well. Now, F sharp minor, if you please."

Yikes! The nun who taught us was always outside, her ear bent to the door, ready to comment to us afterwards on our performance. I think I can date the post-gig slump that I later suffered as a radio broadcaster from the Trinity College exams of the early years: going into the studio, believing myself prepared and always coming out with a sense of having failed. I worked on various radio shows and for years hosted a daily CBC national radio show, *That Time of the Night*. I don't ever recall leaving the studio feeling satisfied. There was always dejection – "It could have been better," some inner voice chastised.

A few weeks after the examinations, report cards arrived. They were small – four-by-six-inch white cards – and were divided into five sections, allowing for comments on each part of the exam. The adjudicators wrote copious comments in a tiny script, in scrawls that make the doctor's prescription look like a monk's careful calligraphy. I use a magnifying glass now to read (probably for the first time) some typical remarks:

> A good speed. The performance caught the wit of the music.
> Kept it going, in spite of slips
> A little more RH [right hand] legato tone needed at times. Same lack of legato in scales in 3rds; but all the rest excellent
> Fluent throughout and clear part-playing. Try to gain more rise and fall in climax. Do make this melody sing out strongly in cantabile tone.

These cards were soon followed by diplomas. One year, in addition to the diploma and card, there came a cash prize. When I cashed the money order, in pounds sterling, it came to about $25, but there was the honour of having won the highest mark in a particular grade in a particular category "throughout all the Empire," we were told. The prize was known as The Guineas, but the diploma reads simply, "Awarded an Exhibition for achievement in pianoforte playing."

In addition to the practical piano and theory exams, there were graded examinations as well for choral singing and choral speech. We were about 110 strong, our glee club, ranging in age from nine to fourteen. We were dressed impeccably in our school uniform, which consisted of long-sleeved white blouses and navy blue serge tunics, with straps in front that formed a V. We had school crests sewn on the left strap and we wore blue and white saddle oxfords, with white ankle socks. We were encouraged to bring to school extra shoes or blouses that could be handed out privately by the nuns to poorer girls, so that we all looked the same. Our deportment was perfect – anything less was unacceptable. Our convent school had zero tolerance policies before that phrase was thought up: zero-tolerance for touching our hair or faces, sniffling, talking or whispering, sneezing. I have spent a good bit of my adult life sneezing – my doctor thinks it's allergies – but it is nothing more than the natural release of all the suppressed sneezes of my childhood. Teachers and parents universally deplore the junior-high age because kids are "impossible." Not only were we not impossible, we were perfect. The secret to achieving that kind of discipline can be found with the nuns who, one hopes, are busily writing guide books for parents.

Most of the girls couldn't read music, so we learned our music "off by heart." We had good ears and good memories. We counted (keeping track of the beats required for each note) without any visible sign we were doing so. I tried using my toes. I'm sure the dramatic toe cramps I suffer today, embarrassing for companions walking along the street with me, come from trying to train my toes to move individually through long melismatic passages (many notes sung to one syllable) of Gregorian chant.

One day I realized toes weren't necessary, that it was easy to count on your fingers discreetly with the Presentation Convent clutch. This was the required hand position for glee club at my school: the left hand turned palm up and cupped slightly, the right hand neatly folded across it palm down with the fingers overhanging the left hand. The two thumbs interlocked, serving two purposes: they held the hands together and they formed a cross reminding us of You Know Who, and how He died. The neighbouring school – the competition, as it were – was run by Mercy nuns; they had their own way of doing things down there. In the Mercy Convent clutch, the left hand was held the same as ours, but the right hand was cupped and placed in the left, palm up. This is a curious distinction and was perhaps a source of great wonder to adjudicators who came from away year after year to judge these choirs. Was the distinction based in some philosophical, religious or social difference, or did it reflect some sort of territorial truce worked out by our founders in nineteenth-century Ireland? In any event, the Mercy bums were singing without the benefit of the cross.

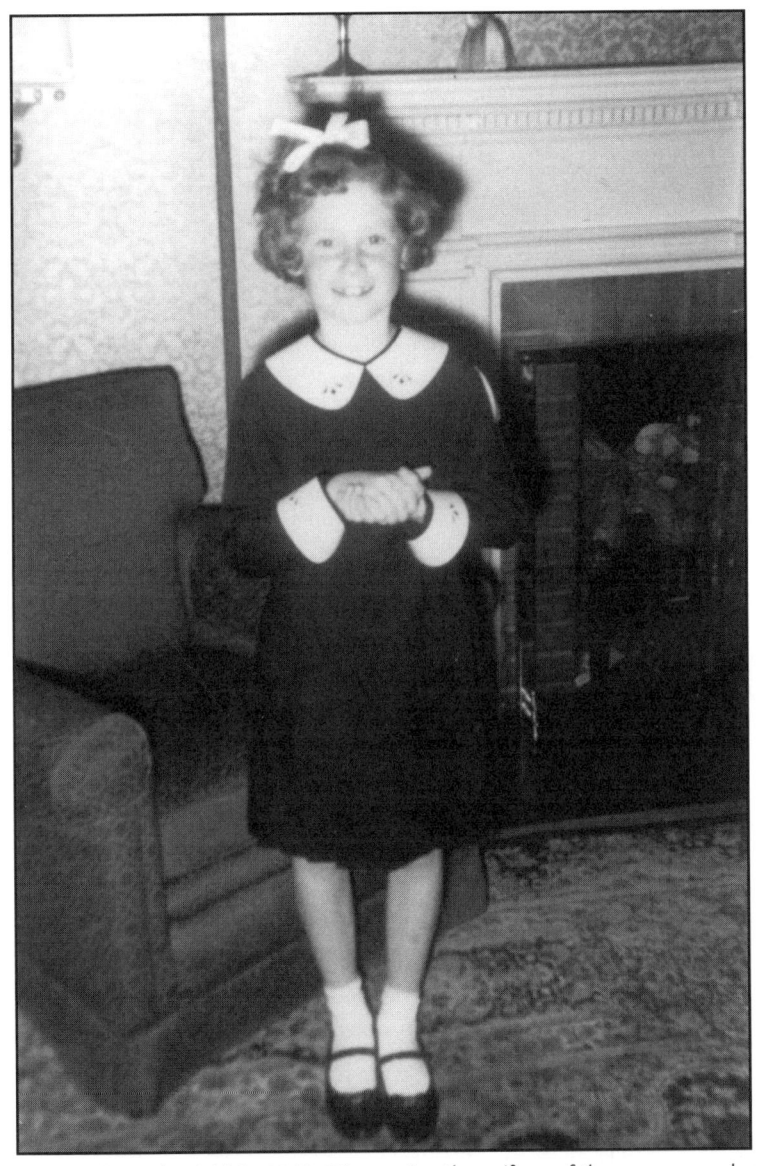

As a convent schoolgirl (c. 1962-63), wearing the uniform of the younger grades. The bow and the school colours on the shoulder suggest readiness for a Trinity College examaination. Note the perfect execution of the Presentation Convent clutch. (Photo by Father John O'Deady C.Ss.R.)

At our Christmas and spring concerts we had parents in the audience; in the music festivals we had competitors and the general public as well. In the Trinity College exams there was an audience of one. We performed in the basement auditorium of our convent school for one person, an examiner from England who sat at a table about half-way down the hall, listened, and wrote. It seems odd, but as with many aspects of childhood, it's only odd in retrospect; it was normal enough at the time. We followed a syllabus with test pieces so, as we stood in our little hall singing for a generic, no-name, stern-looking Brit, other colonial children around the globe stood similarly singing the same pieces, for other generic, no-name, stern-looking Brits. In April or May, with the biting St. John's wind and the inevitable sleet storms reminding us that spring in Newfoundland always mocks the calendar, we would walk to school, descend to the auditorium and practise over and over *Linden Lea* or other pastoral works of Ralph Vaughan Williams.

Finally the great day would come. We stood in the auditorium, scrubbed and brushed, groomed and ready. Our St. John's voices mixed a charming townie lilt with a hint of ancestral Ireland, but we brought to the blend a haughty broadening of our vowels, in deference to those delicate English ears. And then, having never seen an orchard, much less a spring, we would ask with wide-eyed excitement, earnestly, as if we really cared:

> Have you seen an apple orchard in the spring, in the spring?
> An *English* apple orchard in the spring?
> When the spreading trees are hoary
> With their wealth of promised glory
> And the mavis pipes his story in the spring, in the spring.
>
> Have you seen a merry bridal in the spring, in the spring?
> In an *English* apple orchard in the spring?
> When the bride and maidens wear
> Apple blossoms in their hair
> Apple blossoms everywhere in the spring, in the spring.

> If you have not, then you know not in the spring, in the spring
> Half the colour, beauty, wonder of the spring
> No sight can I remember half so precious, half so tender
> As the apple blossoms render in the spring, in the spring.

Did our innocence and charm bring a tear to his eye, our sweetness stir up memories of an evening stroll from his youth? Or did he simply perform his journeyman's duty, commenting on the purity of our vowels, the execution of our consonants, and the musicality of our phrasing?

Trinity College was different from everything else we did. Yes, it was secular – no incense, sanctuary lamps or Latin here. But the absence of the church wasn't the only difference. It was so . . . so English, as opposed to the Irish essence of our day. It was a world intact. Examination papers arrived in big parcels from worlds unknown; they were packaged up and sent back there for grading. Reports and diplomas followed next. There was a detachment about this system, an absoluteness, an infallibility as if it all belonged to a disembodied world. The Land of Oz, Alice's Wonderland, and the North Pole were vivid to us – we knew those landscapes and their people. Trinity College was something vague and foreign, an entity unto itself out there somewhere, like an early version of cyberspace.

These days an adjudicator speaking in front of large groups must entertain, for restless parents with an eye on their watches and a hand on the cellphone ringer wait eagerly for a joke or anecdote to brighten up the business of musical commentary. If the whole team of Trinity College examiners had a scrap of personality between them, we never knew it. Names? Don't know. But twice a year the reports, theory and practical, would come back with the rubber-stamped approval of Mr. Myers Foggin. I picture him snoozing in his London club, an after-dinner port at one side, a cigar burning itself out on the other. His young secretary passes him a ream of diplomas. "Mr. Foggin, sir," the secretary says in a precise Oxbridge accent. "Here are the results for NEWfinlind. The convent did well again, sir."

"Thank you, Edward. And how did Tasmania fare?"

Patsy, Dolly, Gustav, Franz

One day when we were kids and our mother was out, my brother said, "C'mon," and I followed him down to the basement. He hauled a packet of thumb tacks out of his shirt pocket and opened up the lid of the old upright piano.

"Hold it up," he ordered and I, kid sister, lieutenant of fetching and carrying, did as I was told. My brother reached into the workings of the piano and methodically pushed a thumb tack into the felt covering of every hammer.

"There," he said. He sat down and, with honky-tonk freshly painted on the keys, plunked out one of his standards from boyhood piano lessons: "Way Down upon the Swanee River." Was there anything an older brother couldn't do?

We savoured the sound of that honky-tonk piano with the tasty delight of kids who've been bad. Our mother came downstairs from time to time, but the piano didn't interest her. Our secret instrument was hidden in plain view. In my upstairs life as the good kid, I continued practising my melodic minor scales on our shiny Heintzman, newly arrived from Charles Hutton and Sons on Water Street. Downstairs we banged on those bright, clattering keys, colouring our old favourites with a brash new sound. Our family moved out of that house in dribs and drabs, one kid at a time. The piano, bulky, heavy, and squashed into a low-ceilinged basement, was forgotten. Likely, it still sits in the same spot, confounding the new owners. Over the years, I'd hear that clunky honky-tonk tinkle from time to time, but that was as close as I came to country and western music.

It was a Friday night in a suburban living room with friends. Our host was telling anecdotes from his working week. A natural storyteller, he had us all captivated until suddenly he lost me – or I him. It was as if someone had adjusted the volume on the stereo. What had been background noise now shoved aside our affable host, the room's laughter and babble going down with him in an aural heap. I could see his lips moving, his laugh, his grin. I kept my eyes on him, a dopey smile on my face, but I was lost, transfixed, my ear completely given over to a trio of women's voices and their plaintive, seductive crooning: "to know, *know,* **know** him is to love, *love,* **love** him, and I do."

I waited a little, then sidled over to the sound system and fished out the tape. It was called *The Trio*. Three women whose names I'd never heard before – Dolly Parton, Emmylou Harris and Linda Ronstadt. I was thirty-three years old, and country music had reached my soul, for the first time.

I must have heard these singers before, but there's a song that goes, "There were bells all around but I never heard them ringing, never heard them at all, 'til there was you." There is a grain of truth in many corny lines from bad songs that guarantees their immortality. When it came to country music, I hadn't been in receiver mode, not for the style, not for the sentiment. I was a latecomer to love, and you gotta cry before the crying songs can kick in. Now with the aural cataracts gone, country music seemed to be everywhere. It was fresh, new, as if the first country song had been written yesterday. "You don't know Patsy Cline?" said a new friend, incredulous.

"Patsy who?"

And Patsy appeared in my life assuring me that yes, the definition of hell *is* when you've "got the picture and she's got him." Bawl, go ahead, you're justified, she sang. It was all so meaningful and earthy and urgent and immediate. And as Patsy, Dolly and Willie Nelson came in through the door of my heart, out went the lovelorn heroes of Franz Schubert, Robert Schumann and Johannes Brahms. Those poor unfortunates were cooler, aloof. They were pragmatic lovers sitting and totting up their beloved's good points and noting the loss, the way a broker might assess a stock portfolio and regret a small fall in the market. Ah, the German poets wrote, feeding texts to the great song writers: "So-in-so was the joy of my life, now she is gone and I'll never find another, I am left only with misery." It's a philosophical reflection on loss mingled with the requisite nineteenth-century melancholy. Far more localized and acute is the pain of Patsy, wailing about her "faded love."

I listen to a Schubert song describing the frozen tears on the cheek of the abandoned lover; then I hear Patsy Cline's "I Fall to Pieces." The Schubert makes me sad, I sigh a gentle sigh: ahhh, she's gone. I listen to Patsy and wince, I feel it in my gut. Patsy, girl, I'm with you. Why can't he be with *you*, instead of off with that tart?

In another mournful moment, Patsy beats the streets "walkin' after midnight in the moonlight." Her comfort comes in the form of a "weepin' willow cryin' on his pillow." Crying, she hopes, for her. Gustav Mahler, in his *Songs of a Wayfarer*, tells of the hero who went out "in the still night, over the dark heath." Love and sorrow were his company. He encounters a linden tree "which snowed on [him] its blossoms and all, ah, all was well again." There is beauty in the wayfarer's pain. The story unfolds slowly, and Mahler uses the rich colour and possibilities of the orchestra to enhance the tale. The woodwinds respond tenderly to the singer's grief, the funereal pulse of the tympani lends support to his despair. Patsy – all in, all done at 2:02 – gives us a quick kick in the gut. Mahler describes a welcome and honourable misery; Patsy's raucous performance is about raw pain.

Take all those brooding poets with their babbling brooks, shepherds and nymphs, woods and willows, green lush fields, fragrant lilacs and nightingales – the whole lot of it doesn't burn my heart as deeply as the scorch of Patsy's cigarettes. Her "Three Cigarettes in an Ashtray" opens with lovers in a café having a quiet smoke together. The two cigarettes in an ashtray soon become a troublesome three and, ultimately, a lonesome one.

In due course and with the approach of my middle years, ardour and its companion pain have taken their place on the back burner, settled down a little, and Schubert, Mahler and Hugo Wolf are back in their rightful places. Nevertheless, I'm not pitching the Patsy Cline collection – it's filed under U, for "You never know."

I've gone back to "To Know Him Is To Love Him" countless times to sort out why that song, of all the country and western music that must have travelled past my ears, why that song stopped, parked in my brain, then moved on to my heart. Life moment, explains part of it. The same night, I could have been frozen in my tracks by a John McCormack recording of "The Garden Where the Praties Grow." He sings, 'Have you ever been in love, me boys or ever felt the pain? I'd sooner be in jail meself than be in love again.' No, wait: that couldn't have captured me. His tone doesn't match the text. He's pragmatic, cheerful even, as if he's moved on and is cavalier about the memory of his lost love.

But in the queendom of Dolly, Emmylou and Linda, there's no push to move on – no trendy glorification of the healing process. Their subtext is come on in, sit right down, and grieve, grieve, grieve. They're flashing a neon sign that says "Wallow, Wallow." No one in this here territory is going to nag you to "get over it." Their invitation is seductive: embrace the misery, wrap it around you like a warm cloak, and roll in it. They wipe your brow, bathe you with empathy. The song has the universal appeal of the waltz, and the soothing lulling strokes of repetition: "*To* know, *know*, **know** *him is to* love, *love,* **love** *him*." Dolly's not accusatory, just plaintive. "*How blind can he be? Why can't he see that he was meant for* me?" Is he thick, or what? Someday he'll see, she sings, plunking her pack down in the ever burgeoning campground of the delusional. In the meantime, until that illusive day when her unrequited love gets requited, she's at least got the balm of a tender tinkling mandolin and the consolation of the Hawaiian guitar. And, with their close harmony and perfect blend, women's essential comfort team: girlfriends.

Lonesome plucks at the beginning announce sadness. The trio present the situation. They acknowledge grief and temper it with warmth and the mellow hue of the Hawaiian guitar. This is not the grade A, gold card, top of the line pain pack of country and western terrain. This is just a wince, a sliver of splinter under the fingernail, not the wrenching of an amputated arm, not the endless puzzling throb of the phantom limb. It's a watered down, wistful, confessional alloy. It's a lament but not impossibly bleak. She's not yet ready to go over the cliff – she's about six feet back. We, the world weary, know once she gets him she'll lose him, but for the moment we allow her this tender belief and the maudlin mandolin does its best to cheer her on.

Who is this shadowy figure who hovers around the song? Is he worth the torment? Is he unaware of her affections for him, or is he a tease? Blinded to her, or deliberately avoiding eye contact? Why can't she declare herself? A forbidden love? Her pride? The knowledge that he's in love with someone else, that she must patiently wait in line? She's stoic. The one-way love street is enough *for now*; she's satisified just to *know* him. Is this pragmatic or pathetic? The twanging guitars allow us time to mull over the situation. There is a nobility in a private undeclared love but, unlike the heroes of Franz Schubert, Dolly stains the nobility by whining.

The song doesn't end, it fades. We are denied the relief of resolution. Her misery lingers, and we have to carry that. Finally, the singers bail, and we're left with a lone dancer, a one-sided waltz, a waltz for one. And, as one may ponder if a tree falls in an empty woods, is there sound, one may also ask: if one person waltzes, is it a waltz?

"To Know Him Is To Love Him" is a paradigm of country music. Subtlety has been booted out; no transcendence or elevation to art. No speech writer to polish the phrases of the bumbling speaker, just the bumbling speaker. No spin doctor – just the facts, please. *He left. I'm sad.* No fancy sonnets to wrap up the sentiment, hence no deconstruction necessary. No need to hunt through depths, strip away layers to get to the essence or truth. Just a trip down the mine shaft to bring up raw pain. No anaesthetic or palliative measures.

Country and western music is a bulging package of certainties: Love leads to getting together then to splitting up; twosomes lead to threesomes, then onesomes. The message and the medium are so weighted with misery it's a wonder romance has survived, a miracle that marriage as a concept hasn't been wiped off the map of human journeys. A marvel that wedding vows are not seen as ironic. Country and western music is never cautionary. The tenet is: this is how it is.

Country singers are not gracious or subtle; they don't hedge, or couch misery in artifice. They put it out there. Their honesty reaches us, because it's our story too. When Kitty Wells sings "It Wasn't God Who Made Honky Tonk Angels," she sings, "It's a shame that all the blame is on us women." (Context: behind every broken heart there's a man to blame; too many times married men think they're still single.) She lathers the word *shame* with contempt; "shhayymmme," she sings as generations of male listeners wriggle in their chairs.

(Mind you, the most dramatic word painting I've ever heard of that word came from a mezzo soloist singing the aria "He Was Despised" during a performance of Handel's *Messiah* at the Basilica in St. John's. As with all of *Messiah,* the aria is dramatic: powerful text masterfully set. "He was despised and rejected, a man of sorrows, and acquainted with grief." The aria grows dramatically with the line "He hid not his face from shame and spitting." This sounds tame in my treasured recording with Trevor Pinnock and the English Chamber Orchestra. That night in the Basilica, it was ferocious. The mezzo spat. She fired that "shame" around the hall, her consonants and vowels bouncing from soul to soul. Ssssssh-hhhhaaaaammmmme, she sang, as if she were looking through the Romper Room spyglass, as if she'd been appointed by a spiritual adjudicator to prick consciences. The guilty *and* the innocent squirmed.)

Back to the country and western brew: hurt and pain, with a side order of hurt and pain. Life's recipe, really. If your heart is opened wide enough to let in love, there's no keeping out the rest. Country and western music – that monument to man and woman's touching ability to stand in the landscape of love's ruins, and believe again. In the debris, there are uprooted trees, dried-up rivers, orchards ravaged with frost; overhead, dense clouds promise more storms. In the midst stands the bewildered lover who shrinks that scene and sees beyond to a peephole in the black horizon, to a dim flicker, a smidgen of fool's gold, that beckons. She lifts her feet from the muddy mire and begins the familiar march towards love. Country and western music: memorial to the fallen, cenotaph to the optimist, to the ability of humankind to erase the slate, to discard evidence and memory and, intoning the mantra "it'll be different this time," forge on.

Country and western music takes the glamour of romance and trucks it to the dump. The empty truck rattles on the way home. Nothing there but the vapours of cheating, leaving, starting over, cheating, jealousy, vengeance – the usual cycle. It usually stops short of bloodshed. Country and western leaves off with *feelings* of rejection and vengeance. For action you must turn to the arena of opera with its palpable desire and lust, love and hate. Here, midst the arias and cavatinas, quartets and recitatives, you do more than sing of unrequited love or treachery. You fight a duel, fire a gun, stick in the dagger. You write letters, join convents, plant incriminating hankies and scarves, conceal a face with a veil, hide behind a mask, lie, betray your country, mount an army, people your world with tons of illegitimate children who go missing only to reappear at an inopportune time to wreak vengeance in their own way. You stage a play within a play, in which you pretend to murder the victim but oops! The audience knows the smell of real blood. Country and western singers wail about pain, what is, what might have been. They are rueful, more mournful than angry, and they worry more about love than sex. For sex, lust, irrepressible desire, you've got to turn to opera.

In my home office where I work and listen to music (not at the same time), there's a built-in vanity with a stack of drawers on the left and right, but only countertop in the middle; the whole thing sits under a wall mirror. My small stereo system has detachable speakers on each side. The accidental effect is that my listening post looks like an altar. On this musical altar, there are CDs hanging around that never manage to make it back to the main collection. I pulled them once, long ago, to listen for a day or two, and they've resisted refiling. These are not desert island discs, but my altar discs, and include the Bach cello suites, Bach solo keyboard suites, Handel's *Ode for St. Cecilia's Day* (his setting of texts by John Dryden), Haydn's *Stabat Mater*, and singers including Renée Fleming and Sumi Jo. The Dolly Parton CD is in there: Renée, Sumi, and Dolly, piled together quite nicely.

Before that night in my friend's living room when I first heard Patsy Cline, I had sweated, shaken, cried, and quaked alongside opera's tragic heroines: Lucia, Mimi, Violetta, Tatyana, Carmen, Norma. I had loved and suffered with them and others amidst the accoutrements of opera – foreign languages, masked balls, glorious drawing rooms, lonely country paths, charming attics, bohemian cafés, convents, prisons and palaces. That night, Schubert's pining guys on the banks under the willow trees began a slow exodus. As they were disappearing into a painted backdrop, tough chicks from a new world walked in. Those three women – Dolly, Emmy-lou and Linda – reached out a hand and welcomed me into the murky arena of smoky bars, lipstick stains, and cheatin'. Earthy love and its maidservant, misery, presented itself. I embraced country music.

Dinner Music

Only once in my life have I hated music.

I was living in Lausanne, a small sophisticated Swiss city in the French-speaking canton of Vaud. The city rises from the border of Lac Leman, known also as Lake Geneva. The pretty port and waterfront area is called Ouchy, accessible by funicular if you're walking and don't fancy the steep roll down. It is such a Swiss thing to come upon: in a city with no metro or underground, here is this short stretch of track making a tough incline more gentle for walkers. Once I'd seen this, I could never again puff my way up from St. John's Harbour to Rawlins Cross – or in winter slide my way down – without resentment. From Ouchy the ferry travels across the lake to France, to the town of Evian, but it is not sparkling water that the aged Swiss dowagers seek as they fill up the ferry on certain nights. If you can find your way through the wrinkled mounds of caked cheeks, you'll see the glint in their eye: money is the grail. Hours later they return, their suspiciously large purses weighted now with the winnings of vingt-et-un, le poker and la roulette. Occasionally, there is a young companion, someone scarcely noticed on the voyage over, who now has baggage duties on the return trip.

I could see the French Alps from the chair-size balcony off my room, trapping me. The lake, too, was confining: this was too inland for me. I pretended it was the ocean with its promise of freedom. Down the shore from Ouchy is Montreux, home to the jazz festival; along the way is the Castle of Chillon where Byron's prisoner was chained for years. Not far is Vevey where hundreds of people, tons of machinery and a few country cows were working at the noblest of human enterprises. This was not Detroit rolling cars off a conveyor belt; this is the Nestlé's cauldron humming away within nose-shot, bubbling thick, rich chocolate. The thought was cheering. On my balcony I sat and marvelled at the Swiss and their divine triumvirate: money, chocolate, cheese.

There are no clear-cut layers of parallel streets as in St. John's; instead, Lausanne rises from the water in a mound or soft hump. This is a city of church bells, not the tinny electronic eunuchs that grind out hymns from today's churches, but glorious bells colliding with one another in cheerful clusters. And the tiny gaps between the pealing bells give a new clarity to the air around them, so that we hear the city's silence, too. I hadn't heard church bells since my childhood Sundays and St. Patrick's Days. The bells back then announced funerals, too, tolling a single pitch, repeated slowly – a solemn lonesome ring.

And in this charming and beautiful city of Lausanne, I wish I could say I took European lovers and lived in a garret. Alas, I stayed in a residence run by a Swiss German Christian fundamentalist sect. My living arrangements had been made before I arrived. *La Croisée* was a ten-minute walk to the *Conservatoire,* where I was studying flute, piano and *solfege*. It had been billed as a cheap and central student residence in an expensive city. (If you look in the *Guinness Book of Records* under "Fine Print," you will see my name as holder of Most Disastrous Example of Not Reading the Fine Print.) Was it called "Ecumenical Evangelical," or was that my shorthand for a cumbersome foreign name? *La Croisée* provided cheap lodging, mostly for post-secondary students forced to move from their home parishes in the German cantons of Switzerland to the sinful city of Lausanne, usually to attend technical colleges.

The building was Spartan, new by European standards, much like an American-style low-rise from the '60s. It stood out in an unattractive way, dumped on the side of an atypical Lausanne street: a wide avenue with few buildings. The rooms were small and bare. Double rooms were available only to people of the same sex. (They had never heard of same sex couples.) There were sinks in the rooms but hot plates and kettles were *verboten* as they would run up the administration's electricity bill. Those who sneaked in a forbidden appliance uplugged it every morning and hid it in a cupboard in case of a surprise inspection. Cheap was the operative word. Years later, in Barcelona, the natives told me that copper wire was invented by two Catalans fighting over a peseta, but I never saw such tight and ungenerous people as those running this Christian hospice.

Men and women could not visit back and forth between rooms. If you wanted to have a conversation with a guy, you could go down to the main lounge across from *Reception,* and have it there. (A conversation, I mean.) Alternatively, you could sneak out to any room at night as long as you sneaked back in before dawn. Those who broke house rules were evicted; if they were Swiss German, they probably carried home a note to their mother.

The walls and windows were sprinkled with homemade cloth banners and pendants bursting with suns, gold stars, praying hands and crosses. The slogans were written in Swiss German but they weren't hard to figure out: Jesus is Joy, Happiness is Jesus, God Loves Us All. The whole place had the feeling of an elementary school. Adding to this was a fake Sally Field kind of Protestant nun – I used to want to haul the veil off her and say, "Give it up, girl, you wouldn't know a *Stabat Mater* from a *Regina Coeli*, a rosary bead from a Woolworth's necklace." Sister Hilde was the centurion of the front vestibule, posted behind a glass wicket, questioning visitors and handling enquiries. Mail came in through her and she was always eager to sell stamps so that mail could pass *out* through her, too. There were no private phones. Sister Hilde announced incoming phone calls on the intercom; the person summoned would go to a telephone cabin near the reception and wait until the call was put through. To make a call, you gave her the number and went to the same booth. After a few minutes the phone would ring.

"*Mahjahree . . . your telephonica eees . . . now.*" And sure enough, your party would be on the other end of the line. This was true even of a local call. Did she eavesdrop? On the Swiss Germans, I'd say she did. She was young, bubbly, smiling, in your face and generally insipid. There must have been a curfew at night, but I don't remember. She retired around 11:00 and I'm sure I had no key.

The majority of the inmates were Swiss German youths handed over by their families into this mission house for protective custody; what evils the innocuous Lausanne harboured, I could not say. Around this nest of Swiss German wards was a cluster of others – loners, oddballs, misfits – people who at some level understood they could not fend for themselves. For these men and woman, incapable of finding an apartment or taking charge of their lives, this crazy *Croisée* club offered some kind of buffer against loneliness and took care of normal adult responsibilities such as bill paying and grocery shopping. Every one of the non-Swiss Germans had a story; best, I soon learned, not to ask. There was an elderly German woman, Frau Rheinberger, who'd been deposited there when her family took a vacation; they'd be back, they said, but failed or forgot to reclaim her on their return.

There was an Italian woman in her fifties whose hardened leathered look hinted at some uncertain life she'd lived in South America and then in Bahrain. Martina left *La Croisée* every morning and returned every evening, as if she were following the schedule of a working woman, but where she went and what she did, no one knew. She had a hypnotizing way of speaking for hours of many lands, many lovers, like a wizened, weary Scheherazade. I could grasp only some of what she said, but I would sit in her room listening as she passed dreary evenings with her curious recitations delivered in a musical mix of Italian, Spanish and French. Eventually she would wind down and I would come to, out of a daze, as if Peter Pan and Tinkerbell had just dropped me back on the bed after a night flight to parts unknown, mysterious lands. The only residents of the building who spoke English were the American missionaries temporarily parked in Switzerland to learn French before they headed out to proselytize in Ivory Coast. And, as if the roster were not full enough and further to the theory that there is a Newfoundlander everywhere, I regret to admit that I was there, too.

It was at *La Croisée* that for the only time in my life I found myself hating music, (three times a day). There's music not to my taste – Top 40 and disco, although I can accept even these when necessary, say in an aerobics class. There's music that I associate with eternal damnation: if I found myself chained to a chair listening to Celine Dion, I would know I had died and landed in hell. And I have fled from restaurants whose taped music offered the "piano stylings" of Frank Mills, abandoning my date and worse, my duck á l'orange, in *dining interruptus,* as it were. Even then I would not say I hate that music. But at *La Croisée* I despised, with a deep, physical, full-blooded loathing, the handful of Swiss German "hymns" sung before breakfast, lunch and dinner every day. These were not chorales or anthems; they didn't have the majesty or splendour of "How Great Thou Art," or the trusting entreaty of "Eternal Father." No reverence here, no joy, no beauty.

I love to stand in a congregation of strangers and contribute in a small way to a magnificent product. I love to hang around the Estey pedal organ in my old outport house with a crowd of five or six – or three – spontaneously harmonizing "Amazing Grace." I know about the splendour of hymns: I see myself as a nervous school child half-singing, half-whispering my audition piece for a demanding glee club director. My small naked voice, in a register too high for me, tentatively squeaked out "O King of Might and Splendour," a hymn that grew as I grew, turning up as the Passion Chorale to be analyzed, harmonized and modulated at the keyboard in music school. And later it appeared a hymn of might and splendour when I rose in a choir of hundreds to sing the many settings of this chorale as it appears and reappears throughout Bach's masterful oratorio *St. Matthew Passion.*

I love hymns where simplicity and magnificence meet, hymns with their power to move and comfort, a transcendent power that seems unrelated to, and unexplained by, the simple melodies, basic chords and humble text. The most stirring rendition of a hymn that I have ever heard was also the simplest. It was on a lonely outport road on a sunny fallish day. A raggle-taggle band of boys from a neighbouring community had come to give an old veteran a military send-off. These cadets were from an area not well served by the parent organization. These were not supermarket cadets with their perfect army issue and their shiny shoe-boots wanting to sell poppies. These were boys who had only a handful of uniforms among them; they shared, so that everyone had something to show he belonged. Some had cadet hats, but wore hand-me-down pea-jackets; some had pristine army jackets but wore them with sloppy khaki pants. One or two had the perfectly knotted deep black ties, neatly draping the wrong shirts. Their instruments, too, looked doubtful, the clunky keys and slides sluggish and lazy in their response to cold, gloveless hands.

We were near the church, on a hill above the community. There was nothing to see except water and coastline and caves where the eagles nest. There was no one left in the harbour below. The fishing boats had been gone since dawn. All others were here to lay to rest this humble soul who twice a year squeezed his pride and his expanding self into grey flannels and a blue blazer to march in commemorative parades, an array of medals fastened to his chest, a classy beret replacing the salt and pepper hat normally glued to his head. The morning was silent, as if Auden's plea had been granted: the clocks and telephones stopped, the dog silenced with a juicy bone. And into the stark cold morning came warm notes, haphazard shaky sounds that in a moment untangled themselves and settled into "Abide With Me." In the harbour below and the vast bay beyond, there was no sound but these plodding euphoniums unintentionally skewing the harmony here or there, and cornets with their occasional betrayals, the instruments not delivering the pitch the boys' lips were asking for. The phrasing was accidental: no game plan, no musical working out of who'll breathe where to keep the lines flowing. There was no guarantee that the E flat horns would fill in the chords every time or that the tuba would hold his bass note firm and steady and yet . . . and yet, we were moved. At such times, the music, the performance, offers everything we need or want at this moment. It stirs us, as in our hearts we beg: *When other helpers fail and comforts flee, help of the helpless, Lord, abide with me.* On this autumn day, the band shuffles off, continuing to play verse after verse until the hearse stops at a wooded lane. We file through to the cemetery field beyond and wait. Moments later, the tallest boy moves forward and, one foot resting on the mound of fresh clay, stands perilously close to the open grave and sounds taps.

Yes, I can appreciate a hymn, but these *Croisée* spectacles were not hymns; they were silly songs sung by grown-ups acting like kindergarten tots, except not as good. It was like Swiss German *Skin-*

namarink-y-dinky-doo, as musically rewarding as *Mary had a little lamb*. Nursery rhymes are charming, but they belong to childhood. Imagine going to a friend's house to be greeted by your host saying: Look here, before cocktails and dinner, how about a round of Little Sally Saucer?

The refectory was fitted out with tables of six. We stood behind our chairs before our meals while the evangelicals did their thing. "When I smile the Lord smiles with me," the little Pollyannas sang in their gruff unmusical language. Others joined in, except the table of deaf boys sent to Lausanne to attend a special school. They, like me, stood mute.

It started in my toes, then spread up through my calves as far as my liver, then farther, this crawling visceral anger. How could an innocuous cluster of B flats and C sharps turn my body to fossilized rage? What was stored in those quarter notes and eighth notes? Their music was a symbol of that reduction of humanity that characterizes fundamentalism, the life-denying simplification of the breadth of human experience. God's good, we're good, everything's great. For you maybe, baby, but there's a lot of life outside your circle. I stood there, captive, as they vocalized their self-satisfaction, this safe little club of God's select. They smiled and clapped and basked in arrogance. They were unassailable, welcoming defiance and skepticism because it swelled their sense of righteousness. They smiled because *I was going to hell, and they weren't*.

I arrived late for meals as often as I could. There was a McDonald's down the hill across from the railway station and I went there when I was desperate, but this was a waste of money as my meals were prepaid at the *Croisée*. Besides, if you didn't show up for a meal, they would suspect you were eating in your room and that might lead to a tough inspection which would reveal a hair dryer, kettle or other contraband.

We were summoned to meals by a dinner bell, not a single gong but a slow arpeggio, a broken major triad: do, mi, sol. I was like Pavlov's dog, starting to feel sick as soon as I heard the summons. Several years later I was running to catch a train through *La Gare* in Barcelona when I heard the exact same sound, the broken major triad; it's used there to catch people's attention before announcements of arrivals and departures. I dropped my suitcase, and fought nausea for a few minutes before I could collect myself, pick up my luggage and carry on running.

On Saturday and Sunday mornings I set my clock for five minutes before the breakfast gong was due to sound. I would get out of bed and run the tap in my sink to block the sound. Then back to sleep, having spared myself the misery at least twice a week.

I was a misfit in a band of misfits. I could have left at any time, but my European sojourn was to be for only six months. My walk to the *Conservatoire* was along a narrow cobblestone road with two chocolate shops en route. My morning stroll at dawn to French classes at *L'Eurocentre* brought me over a high bridge that gave a breathtaking view of the city, the lake and the French mountains across the water. The mornings were cool but I would pause to watch the pale white-gold light slowly take over a grey winter sky. At night at the *Palais Beaulieu*, a short, safe bus ride away, I could see the Beja Ballet dance Ravel's *Bolero*, and the *Orchestre National de France* play the works of Brahms, Mahler, and Schumann. I could hear Haydn's *Creation* in the *Cathedrale*. I would not give it up. I knew the young make sacrifices to study in Europe, but not like this! I had been prepared to wilt in a garret on bread and wine, but I was starving on sauerkraut in a mission house. My calendar from that period records the concerts I saw and the meals I dreamed of. (The list is typical of a Newfoundlander coming of age in the '70s, torn between two culinary styles: beef stroganoff, brandied chicken breasts, jig's dinner, shish kebab, lasagne, cod tongues.) I thought I'd be working my way through a line of bearded monosyllabic lovers – they'd be intellectuals if only I spoke their language. Instead, I was warding off evangelical pamphleteers.

They made one concession: I could use the piano *free*. The piano was in the chapel, a place too modern and sparse to feel holy to me. The chapel was attached to the residence and was opened only on weekends. During the week it was stark and cold. And dark. I could use the piano, but no one mentioned anything about firing up the electricity. I'm jumpy, the kind of person who rises a foot off the floor if approached suddenly. There were two doors in the chapel, one to the street and one to the residence, so there was no way I could position the piano so that I could see both doorways. Every few measures I'd stop, thinking I'd heard something – it took half an hour to get through the *Minute Waltz*. But I went every day, working on the pieces I was studying at the *Conservatoire,* figuring out fingering, trying to memorize Bach *Inventions.* Scared of an unexpected pounce, half-frozen and snivelling with self-pity, I would sob my way through Chopin's *Raindrop Prelude,* feeling the passion of Georges Sand and Frederic Chopin, smelling the warm Spanish winds of their Majorca.

I had come to Europe to live among foreigners, sit in cafés drinking absinthe, mix with artists and students. But where were Rodolfo and Mimi and Puccini's other Bohemians? Who would walk into the chapel, and place my poor shivering hand in his, singing: *Che gelida manina, Mahjahree,* put your frozen hand here, Marj, I'll warm it up for you. No one, it seemed. Gloomy silence met the end of every piece. And the student prince? He was meant to be outside my window serenading me before he'd whisk me off to a night of cavorting in the taverns. The only nocturnal sounds I heard from the street came from an open window in another part of the building: prayer services, in Swiss German, and yes, they began and ended with "hymns."

I extricated myself after six months. I was like a landlubber touching ground after a harsh voyage, the rough seas mercifully fading as I walked that first block. I breathed in the soaring air of freedom and began to sing, celebrating my release, and theirs.

The Disappearing Concert

*H*e's got his hand on his cock, the guy on my left, and the kid behind is kicking my seat. On my right two seats over, a Max Factor poster girl gives off a mix of mousse, styling putty, perfume, and chemically enhanced dental floss. I can't see all that, but I deduce it from the distinct aromas travelling in front of my nose, as if a parade of trolls is toting chunks of lipstick and tiny patties of rouge. In front of me, a man with too much head, a woman with too much hair. Somewhere in the vicinity, gum chewing and lozenge sucking compete in oral Olympics; nearby, a set of molars chomps its way through hard candy. I ask myself, once again, why have I come?

"Good evening, ladies and gentleman, my name is . . . I'd like to welcome you on behalf of the Kaboto Club of . . ."

Shoulda stayed home. Shoulda bought the CD. Here I am, again, at that fatal contemporary phenomenon, tangentially related to music: the concert. I hauled my bones out here tonight when I could have sprawled on the couch listening to an old CD, or a new CD with the money I'd have saved. I could have had a lazy dinner, wine, coffee, followed by pee-breaks whenever I wanted them, with no queuing. At the end of the evening, instead of sloshing my way to an icy car, I could have walked the few steps to bed.

I study my neighbours carefully. We are a little octet unknown to each other except by our snorts, sneezes and smells. Two hours with these people – can I do it? The cock guy is none of my business: it's not my hands on his cock or his hand on *my* . . . The head-and-hair team in front are talkers – she leans towards him to whisper, a minute later, he has a thought he can't hold. Back and forth they go, I dodge between them trying to find a window to the stage. Before long, I'm swaying, slowly but regularly, a human pendulum. The kid behind is kicking with a pattern; soon we've got a little rhythm section on the go. A glee club song from childhood comes back to me. *Tick-a-ticka-tock, my guitar softly playing, Tick-a-ticka-tock, the music swaying.* The gum chewer, the candy chomper, the mint sucker – is it coincidence or are they working at this? We're doing well. *Tralala-tralala.* A sneezer joins us, right about where the bass drum would be; he's steady and reliable, his sneezes perfectly paced. A nose blower – with an elaborate two-toned blow, one pitch for each nostril – provides the support of the tympani. We need a snare drum to complete this trap set and we get it: five seats over, one row ahead, restlessness overtakes an old lady; she taps her program. *Tick-a-ticka-tock, the dancers swaying, come and dance a gay measure with me.*

On stage, the MC is rambling. I hear the words "corporate sponsors."

"The concert could not go ahead tonight if it we're not for Petro Canada, Husky Oil, the Royal Bank, federal and provincial governments, NewTel, Newfoundland Power, ACOA, Enterprise Newfoundland and Labrador, and other granting agencies such as LIP, LAP, SLIP, SLAP, FLIP and FLOP." He chooses acronyms over the clumsy nomenclature of these government inventions.

"We are grateful that each of these agencies has been able to send a representative tonight, to bring greetings. I know you'd like to show your appreciation while I invite these good people to join me on stage. Come on out here, folks — ."

He babbles on as a covey of suits – and one skirt – shuffles onto the stage. They bunch together. The junior ones look as if the dividers around their office cubicles have fallen, exposing them. The senior ones hunger for the safety of the corporate boardroom where at least they know how to pronounce all the words. The politicians beam; they are at the ready – a lot can be said in one or two minutes, and with an election nearing, every opportunity counts. If they get one new vote here tonight, the evening is worth it.

"You can't campaign during a *concert*, Dad," I once heard a sixteen-year-old son tell his father, a minister of the crown.

"If you ever grow up and pluck that earring out of your nose, you might actually learn something."

Uriah Heep, representing the orchestra, slinks to the podium. There is a mini love-in between cheque giver and cheque taker. I squirm. Twelve minutes after eight and not a note played, not a syllable sung. The orchestra players look grumpy, skeptical. A petulant oboist cleans his instrument methodically, determinedly, hauling a variety of colourful feathers through the bore. ". . . and our company has shown consistently – in fact we are a clear leader in this field – that we believe in the arts. I know some of you out there get a little uncomfortable around the" – he pauses and smiles – "'artsy-fartsy scene,' but the arts in this province today are worth more than $200 million. I'm including tourism here."

Around me our accidental combo is occupied, working its way through our ad hoc score. At 8:15 the concert begins. The restless crowd has settled down. All's well in the first short orchestral overture. Then the centrepiece, the moment we've come for: a setting by Alessandro Scarlatti of the *Salve Regina*:

> Hail! Holy Queen, mother of mercy,
> Hail! our life, our sweetness and our hope
> To thee do we cry, poor banished children of eve,
> To thee do we send up our sighs, mourning and weeping
> in this valley of tears.

The soprano and mezzo are exquisite; their voices are my launching pad, springing me out of the concert hall and into a fresh new kingdom of wonder, ecstasy. FLIP and FLOP are forgotten. My flight is cut short by the guy on my right. He's ansty. I've never seen anyone so excited about a *Salve Regina*. He's wriggling, as if he's anticipating something extraordinary. All right, so he knows the piece. Hold on, buddy, that exquisite moment of dissonance, that bittersweet wistful crunch, that longed-for resolution, that secondary dominant pivot chord that rolls us into a new key – it's coming, yes, but hold on. I have to stop myself from patting his hand.

Salve Regina, sing the soloists, drawing out the vowel in a glorious melismatic passage, the *aahhhhaaaahhhhahhh* lasting forever as if there is no ending to this phrase, as if they want to eternalize this one word, give their lives to this one syllable, this one vowel sound extended over dozens of notes, dozens of beats. It will stop, but perhaps they believe it should go on forever: Hail Queen, hail! Hail! – a greeting of worship, of adoration, of supplication. They nurture that one vowel sound, they loll in it, like sun worshippers on a southern beach. Sahhhhhhhhhhhllveeeeeehhhhhh.

And now as the melody descends one note at a time, the singers, too, seem to descend slowly, carefully, as if, dressed in velvet gowns, they are following one another down a regal staircase, following closely, cautiously, so as not to tread on each other's hem. Their blend is perfect, their nuances matched. They are flawlessly paired as if they are sharing one gown; they travel closely, one small step forward, the other close behind, each taking a definite step, neither pushing nor pulling the other, while the tips of their fingers at the ends of long-gloved arms gently touch, a connection so delicate it may be an illusion. We sit spellbound.

The orchestra begins the next section with more movement and energy. My neighbour moans. He's making and unmaking tight fists. He's tense, angry. The music can't be doing this. Does he know one of the soloists? Only the vengeance of an erstwhile lover could explain this. He's bitter. The piece is dramatic, with emotional highs and lows.

Ad te clamamus, to thee we cry.

I swear he's crying. He feels their pain.

I feel the tension slipping out of him, and the whole row seems to relax. He's settling down, so we're settling down. I sneak a peek – he's smiling. Here's a guy who knows his Latin – his spirits have picked up with the change in text. There's not a murmur out of him now, not a fidget, he sits quietly; whatever was eating him is settled. He relaxes: he *grins*. It's impressive the effect the music has had on him. Now comes a tender duet, and the warm sounds of the organ, vaguely heard in the continuo, seem to have soothed him.

What a delicate little sugar plum – wouldn't want to sit next to him through the Fauré or Mozart *Requiem*. He'd never survive.

I hear him gulp.

Ad te suspiramus, to thee we sigh. Yes, it is moans and groans I'm hearing. The orchestra finds its stride, marching along at a contolled pace, definite. He grabs my arm.

Jeeze.

Et Jesum, the soloists sing, *Et Jesum.*

Blessed is the fruit of thy womb.

I could swear I hear the F word.

Benedictum fructum

"F . . . 'em," he whispers so loud I'm sure the usher will come. "*Shit!* I don't believe it. The Leafs! They won! Wiped out Anaheim."

O dulcis virgo Maria! Oh sweet Virgin Mary.

The kicking kid, the nose blower, the mint sucker, the candy chomper – my restless off stage band – they lean towards him, the hair-and-head couple turn back. My neighbour on the left – the hand-on-the-cock-guy – spreads himself across my lap to hear the impassioned whispers coming from my neighbour on the right.

"Who got the winning goal?"

He was a hero, like a messenger back from Troy with news of the advancing army, swelling with importance as the villagers, greedy for breaking news, badger him. The soprano and mezzo soloists carry on, nearing their consoling conclusion to the Scarlatti setting. We, the devoted slaves of sacred music, we who, in spite of every physical discomfort, the accidental conspiracy surrounding us, we who climbed aboard the proffered cloud and basked for a time in another dimension, we who entered a world above and beyond, we grab the last moments, savour the dying phrases.

O clement, oh loving, oh sweet virgin mother.

Buddy's fingers rummage through his thick hair; he moves his hand quickly into his coat pocket where I now notice the tiny Walkman cord hanging out.

On stage, as the soloists leave, one of the orchestral musicians, a gawky boy who fancies himself an entertainer, walks to the podium and a gives a seven-minute introduction to what turns out to be a four-minute piece. Near me, during the performance, a young man keels over. We fuss over him, trying to decide if it's a simple fainting, heart attack, or insulin shock. Crumpled in the squeeze between the chair and floor, he whispers something to me. His last confession? The location of the key to his safety deposit box? What, tell me, I urge. I finally get it: he explains that when he turns off the ringer on his cellphone, this activates a body vibrator. He'd never tried it before tonight. The orchestra is paused on a held chord; the audience is silent, as if they have finally noticed there's somebody up on that stage. Now, it's as if the audience has been caught out, caught misbehaving and the conductor has decided he's not proceeding one semiquaver until everyone is still. No one stirs. And in that hair's breadth before the conductor releases the pause – that first delicious moment of peace in the hall – a wrist-watch beeps, reminding the wearer of some commitment too important to forget, not important enough to remember. A woman who has to leave early crawls over seventeen of us to get out. And so it goes until, an hour later, we are released into the frosty parking lot and, mercifully, allowed to return home.

The above, dear reader, is an amalgam of various concert experiences, with some anticipated horrors thrown in. *Yet*, I cannot give up the concert habit, for who but a fool would walk away from a cheap miracle?

The concert: an hour before, in an alley out back, solitary figures saunter through the stage door. Some are young with purple hair; some have weariness etched on their forehead, an invisible bumper sticker that reads: rather be home. The loads they carry vary, from soft leather bags smaller than a notebook computer to body bags lugged over their shoulders. In corners backstage, in halls and shared dressing rooms, they open those small coffins, cozy resting places of gold or red velvet, where the piccolo or trumpet lies. They unload their gear: pieces of brass hammered into odd shapes, blocks of wood tenderly carved into objects of beauty, feathers and rags for cleaning, oil for resistant valves and cranky keys, cigarette papers for sticky pads, resin for bow hair, cushions and rests for chins and shoulders, spools of colourful twine for oboe reeds, stools for the bassists, discreet mutes parked on stringed instruments, stubby mutes for the brass. And as precious as their instruments are the reams of paper tucked under their arms, paper with lines and squiggles and dots – a secret code loaded with the world's richest cargo.

All that gadgetry and gear, the tackle of music, that transforms the ordinary into the extraordinary. Together, workers with their talents and tools build the concert – that light rail system that circles the globe carrying tunes and harmonies thousands of miles, hundreds of years. They perform their trick of re-creation – that mystical moment easing a delivery into your ear. The direct line: Mozart at the end of the speaker phone, Schubert sharing his glorious tunes, Bach himself before you, transcending all that has happened today and yesterday, travelling through the breadth of lives lived, stretching across all human suffering and glory and achievement and pain, crossing it all and, at the same time, embracing it all. The concert rolls in, carrying ideas, emotions, challenges and pleasure – the train with its free pass: *get on board*. The coach circles humanity, offering rides because a muse visited a genius, a genius was compelled to create, a language evolved to record the ideas, and the skills to read and interpret have been passed on. The concert is nothing but a collection of men and women, a language, and the spark from the composer's brain, the light from a lone soul. No technology is required to reproduce the sound – nothing electronic or artificial; no computers or fibreoptics, no flash or splash or wild lighting. Drama yes – but drama contained in notes and rests. The concert is the wine where, before, there was only water; it's food for the multitudes from a basket of bread and a plate of fish.

And we, the audience, are part of it. We have to get it right – stifle rustles, contain coughs, deny ourselves the comfort of sucking, chewing or mewling. And when it works, time and place are suspended, the ordinariness is gone, and Ben Heppner, yes Mr. Ben Heppner, is singing "Roses of Picardy," sending it right here to seat F 28, this great man with this small song singing for *me*. There is no one else in the hall now, no coughers or chewers, no hot or cold air. Just singer, song and me.

> Roses are shining in Picardy,
> In the hush of the silvery dew.
> Roses are flowering in Picardy,
> But there's never a rose like you (Marjie Doyle).

> And the roses will die with the summertime,
> And our hearts may be far apart,
> But there's one rose that dies not in Picardy
> 'Tis the rose that I keep in my heart (Marjie Doyle).

He sings so softly I feel my heart. There is nothing now outside this private triangle: a warm, purring voice; a tender melody; and the rose (me). He sings as if each note and word have been lifted out of the phrase, caressed, polished with a chamois, and tenderly reshelved on the melodic line. By some sleight of hand, he seems to make no effort, but small jewels spill out. The artist's tools are hidden, the skill and craft; we see only this finished product. We see and hear his ability to land with perfection on every note and consonant, his judgment to linger on a vowel. We suck in nuance, subtlety, and beauty in this small work of art.

And this, too, is the magic: that we believe this is the first song Ben Heppner has ever sung, the only song, because *he could not do it twice*, could not bring such contained energy and gentleness and care to this song if it were not the first time. He could not sound like this if he travelled the globe singing night after night; no, he could not sustain that. This surely is a one-off, his first time, his only time. That is part of the spell, the eclipse of all other musical experience. There is no memory of an earlier song, no hint that another will follow, no acknowledgment that all around the world tonight there are thousands of songs being sung on stage and off, into lovers' ears, on radios and in nurseries to nodding children. No: there is only this one song.

And no thought that on other nights, in other places, this powerful Heldentenor (tenors who fill the big heroic roles in German opera) climbs all over the Wagnerian repertoire; we don't remember that as he steps into this one song, as if every piece of music is equally worthy, deserving of his musicianship. The democracy of it – no snobbery or discrimination – bringing all he has to this one piece, this one time. There is no sense he has reduced his great self to this small song, but that this small song has been elevated by him. The hall is frozen. We've stopped breathing. There is nothing outside this melody, sung to me, Marjie Doyle in F 28, as if it were a command performance and I some great majesty.

That is the concert. Or the solo recital where a small man walks across a large stage to a lone prop – the handsome glistening Steinway, its eager lid up, welcoming. When Vladimir Ashkenazy sits at the keyboard, Beethoven in his head, Beethoven in his heart, when he plays those three sonatas, there is nothing else. We have shifted from a St. John's hall into a separate country, leaving behind the bundle of incipient sneezes, explosive coughs, itches that need scratching. The ticket stubs in our pockets – damp and crumpled by fidgeting fingers – they gave access to the anteroom, but Beethoven is the real ticket, the real ride. And we are gone now to every corner of our humanity. *How could the guy next to me be listening to a hockey game?*

Or sitting in a Swiss concert hall, the Palais Beaulieu in Lausanne, hearing the American pianist Murray Perahia play Schumann's *Piano Concerto in A Minor*. The audience holds its collective breath, releasing it amidst applause thirty-one minutes later. Even the silent space between the first two movements had been tenderly protected by the listeners. A whisper travels the hall and within minutes it seems all of us – even foreigners hearing the news in mumbled, hushed French – have gotten the heads-up that tomorrow night in the neighbouring town of Vevey, Perahia will shed the orchestra and wander deeper into the puzzle of Robert Schumann: he will perform the *Davidsbündlertänze* in a solo recital. And the next night, the normally lonesome railway platform is filled as we patrons from the night before impatiently await the train, rushing to get the seat on the railway car that will allow us to be first off, first to the box office, lest the concert sell out. Good manners, Swiss reserve and traditions of queuing are threatened because the stakes – admission to the recital – are high. *That* is the concert experience. Or when you find yourself seated in Orchestra Hall in Chicago, Georg Solti is conducting the Chicago Symphony and, as if you deserved it, Mstislav Rostropovich is walking on stage; in a moment his cello will sing the Dvorak concerto.

I wade through the roster of concerts mostly listening to politicians, opportunists, and corporate sponsors. Musicians, sometimes dry, sometimes shy, explain, entertain, describe, tell anecdotes. Underlying this is the belief that people don't want to hear classical music, so you have to brighten up a dull evening any way you can. Others justify the long rambles as "education." Save it for a matinee, I say, or a night course. When the concert hall turns into a classroom, the concert turns into a lesson, shoving out the magic. I don't know if the concert has disappeared elsewhere, but in these parts it began to happen within the last ten years. Now on a blustery winter night (any night from November to May), I make up my own concert series. In the comfort of my scent-free living room, silent, remote from oil executives passing cheques to fawning recipients, I curl up on the couch, and flick "play."

And yet: I can never forget. Leaving the concert hall in Barcelona, spilling out onto the *Ramblas*, into its rich Mediterranean life, the *Ramblas* where opulence marches side by side with penury. Patrons in furs trip over the homeless, as Catalunya's finest dodge the beggars, the nursing mother and her half-clad child. I head up the *Ramblas* and descend into the metro. It's almost empty at this late hour. Any delay at the concert, even an encore, might have made us too late for this last train of the night.

Only two of us stand on the chilly platform. The old man in the tuxedo looks worn out. He holds his instrument tight to his chest; it's probably his greatest asset, this violin. He's a workman in a uniform, on permanent night shift, as performers are. If he lives far, he probably hung around a bodega between the afternoon rehearsal and tonight's show, rather than ride the train home. He will play this program again tomorrow night and the next and the next; if it's an opera he might play the same music for a month. He doesn't earn a lot, and along with rehearsals, he still has to practise every day, to get the licks down. I look into his eyes. He plays hundreds of hours of music, working six nights a week, eleven months of the year. He is bone weary, but not depleted; something carries him beyond sore shoulders, worn-out eyes, headaches, worries. Something sustains him. Tonight, he was *it:* he and another like him and another and another, and the *chef d'orchestre* in front and the sheaves of papers with their loaded hieroglyphics. They are the tricksters, the wand-wavers who weave the elements into one new whole, into something that exists for an hour or two, and then disappears without a trace. They are the concert.

"*La solo – que usted a tocado – me encanta.*" I fumble to tell him I loved his playing. I want to be specific, but can't retrieve the vocabulary. A lame "*muy bien*" sputters out.

He shrugs. His eyes focus far from mine.

"*Es la musica. Siempre la musica.*"

We are silent.

"*Y ustedes tambien*," he nods at me. You too, he acknowledges and through the thicket of half familiar Spanish comes in broken English: "There must – to be – peoples. Peoples to hear."

So, responsible "peoples" that I am, inevitably, after a run of solitary nights lazing at the home stereo station, I am lured back to the concert hall, savouring remembered marvels, and greedy for more.

A Chorus Girl Away

Music is a hobby that travels.

My first stage appearance outside my native land took place at Mount Allison University in Sackville, New Brunswick. Because I was raised in a household in which we still thought of Newfoundland as a country, I considered this my Canadian debut. I would like to say I'd been invited there or that I was on tour. In fact, it was Fun Night at a summer music camp. All the other "acts" were non-nation specific; the kids performing together weren't from the same place and didn't feel they had to make a statement. They mostly performed skits and campfire songs. But there is something about Newfoundlanders, as if there exists inside us a system of invisible magnets that exerts a pull when we come within a certain radius of one another, as if we're all hooked up to some version of a fishfinder.

There we were at Mount A and it was as if a siren heard only by Newfoundlanders had been activated and presto! we were in one place at one time, with an unstated notion that there should be official representation from our country. Standing among us kids was a huge man dressed in black pants and white t-shirt, a pleasant fellow with a booming voice who had a friendly teasing manner with the boys. The boys introduced him as "Br" (pronounced burr), the universal form of address used by Catholic boys for the Christian Brothers who taught them. He was on campus taking summer school and, yes, he knew how to dance. He was easily six feet tall and 250 pounds, but relatively light on his feet. At least he knew the steps. From that moment until the great night, we rehearsed in every spare moment until we got the "Lancers" (a popular Newfoundland quadrille) down. In my memory I try to convince myself that I ended up the piano player (the tune was "I'se the B'y"); I was a self-conscious, clumsy kid and would have entered any pact to spare myself going on stage *dancing*. We girls wore bright red skirts and white blouses, the boys wore white shirts and grey pants. I marvel at this now. Parents today could only wish for kids so innocent that they go off to a co-ed camp – a big deal for us because we went to separate schools – and, rather than drink, smoke dope or screw one another, they get up on the stage in matching outfits and do the bloody Lancers!

The idea of carrying my patriotism abroad seemed natural and a few years later I found myself, solo this time, performing the "Ode to Newfoundland" on my knees in my university cafeteria.

When I had arrived on campus the first day at Mount St. Vincent University in Halifax, I knew no one. I was by myself in the frosh registration line. When it came time to have my photo ID made, I was asked my name. Then:

"Middle name?"

My middle name was Marie but when I opened my mouth, "Joseph" came out.

(It was like an unwanted visitation from Mr. Bean.)

"Your middle name is Joseph?" How is it that all those sucky seniors who end up "working" registration seem as if they're auditioning for jobs with the gestapo? They have that air of condescension exuded by women who work in high-end dress shops when someone other than a perfect size eight comes in.

"Yes." I was definite. (My confirmation name *is* Joseph. I had wanted to honour the Holy Family but the priest said I already had "Marie," which was really Mary, and I could hardly take Himself.)

So moments later, although I did not yet know what use I could make of it, I had an official university photo ID card with the name Marjorie Joseph Doyle. It seemed a good thing to have.

Later during that first semester, in the university cafeteria one day stories were going around the table, and I threw out, casually: "In Newfoundland, every baby born after Confederation is named after Joey Smallwood."

There were a few guffaws but I could lie. My brother and I had perfected the art of lying in childhood on a need-to-lie basis involving, say, cigarette smoking or broken windows. I created a few good stories to back up my claim.

"You're kidding," said the gullible.

"I don't believe you. That's ridiculous," said the sophisticate from Montreal who'd been banished to an all-girls, nun-run university by her parents, who thought that removing the distraction of boys would help focus her grades.

I pulled out my student ID, as impressive a document as any of us had at that age and there I was: Marjorie Joseph Doyle. In the silence, with even the skeptic caught off guard, I forged on, letting myself be guided by Gilbert and Sullivan's Lord High Executioner of Titipu, adding "corroborative detail . . . to give artistic verisimilitude to an otherwise bald and unconvincing narrative."

"Well, I never really do this, but once a day we're supposed to face Newfoundland, kneel and sing a verse of the 'Ode.'" And down I went, singing the first line or two before one of the gestapo came charging towards me. Probably thought I was on mescaline when, in truth, I was locked into a childish sense of fun, left over from a girlhood in a convent school.

The ability of people to believe anything about Newfoundland because of their ignorance of it offers unlimited opportunities. It reached its heights for me later in Macomb, Illinois, after a music theory classmate at Western Illinois University learned I was from Newfoundland. "Wow," he said. "Your English is fantastic."

"Thank you," I said.

"So, what's your first language, anyhows?" He talked like Howdy-Doody.

"Latin." It sort of was: I spent so much time in church that *"Et cum spiritu tu tuo"* rolled off my tongue as easily as eeny-meeny-miny-moe, and made about as much sense.

"Jeeze, I didn't think they still *spoke* Latin anywheres. Is it, like, the official language?"

"Sort of. There are so many Catholics there and they spend so much time in church, it just turned into the vernacular – accidentally."

"Wow."

But mostly when I played or sang away from home, it was not Newfoundland music. In Illinois, I played alto sax in a stage band and sang with the university choir in Arthur Honegger's *Le Roi David* (King David). In Madison at the University of Wisconsin, I sang Bach's oratorio *St. Matthew Passion,* a performance so long we had a supper break during it. In Barcelona, I sang with the *Orfeó Català de Barcelona*, the house choir of the *Palau de Musica,* pride of the Catalans, the repressed people of Generalissimo Franco. They'd been forced to suppress their language and culture during his long *dictadura*. The regime ended with his death in 1975; ten years later, around the time I arrived, the Catalans were basking in their language and culture. I felt at home there, aligned with them in some inexplicable way, and comfortable because the Catalans and the Spanish are warm and easy people. When I reflect on my two years in Barcelona, I think I was *saved* by singing in the choir.

We rehearsed two nights a week, late, as the Spanish eat late. Our rehearsals began at 9:00 and ended at 11:30. Afterwards, I walked to a nearby square where taxis hung out. The uneasiness I felt walking in the downtown late at night, the cab rides, and entering the empty apartment at midnight – my mate worked late – were incidental, next to the joy of singing.

Language wasn't a problem. Choristers are used to singing in languages other than their own. The director, one of the myriad expatriate Brits living in Spain, conducted the rehearsals in his fledgling Catalan. He spoke in slow simple sentences with a pronunciation mystifying for the native speaker, but perfect for the foreigner; with a smattering of French, Latin and the Spanish I was starting to learn, I could get his drift. Besides, a good conductor communicates about phrasing or articulation as much by gesture or example as by explanation. There was always the fear I'd miss an announcement of a performance or a change in dress code, but in those cases someone would lean over and whisper to me in slow, careful Spanish.

We sang in Catalan once only, at a Christmas concert. We had finished our program of standard repertoire and I was expecting to leave the stage when the choir began singing music unfamiliar to me. These were well-known Catalan carols such as "El Noi de la Mare" (these days I seem to hear this pretty carol everywhere). The music had not been passed out, or practised, or mentioned. The conductor simply led the choir into an annual tradition. I stood mute in the middle of eighty people; I couldn't even "mouth the words" as the proud Catalans sang. We also sang in English once, when we sang Mendelssohn's *Elijah*. It was odd to be sitting in a rehearsal being drilled on your own language, but I didn't dare walk out, because the coach was a Brit who probably thought my English was unacceptable anyway.

We hit the road a couple of times a year. Once, we travelled to Aosta in the Italian Alps just before Christmas. We flew to Geneva and then bused our way up the snowy mountain into the cool dry air, driving from late afternoon with its fading winter light, to darkness. There was time before the performance to stroll the streets of this quiet Alpine town. We walked in bunches, a string of six or seven of us filling up streets that seemed to have no cars. Snow was falling, not sideways as it does in Newfoundland, carried on a harsh wind, but straight and regulated as if above us a theatre technician roamed a catwalk controlling the flow of snow: the rhythm was steady, the flakes consistent, and newly arrived snow remained white.

It was a village of tiny shops. The store fronts were not the sweeping windows of the city with life-sized mannequins and over-sized Christmas gifts. These windows were made up of small squares of glass, squeezed together; the products and scenes displayed were tiny and detailed as if Swiss precision had crossed the mountains. The shops gave off a warm intimate light, from old-fashioned single bulbs in the ceiling, rather than fluorescence. I had seen towns like this, in the pages of children's story-books. Every second shop seemed to be a tearoom where well-dressed Europeans sipped cocoa, sucked on homemade confections rolled in icing sugar, letting chocolate melt in their mouths. These were the last days before Christmas. Far off in the cities, the streets and department stores would be madness; here, there was a rare stillness and beauty under clear dark skies. Wandering around the streets with their promise of Christmas, I felt distant from the others, knowing that when we returned to Spain, they were going home to the harried pleasure of family Christmases – they were full of those false complaints about the season's chores. I'd be staying in my downtown Barcelona apartment, trying to cobble together a Christmas the way expatriates do.

But loneliness evaporates as we climb the steps of the ancient stone church where we are to perform Haydn's oratorio *The Creation*. Here we are: a Catalan Choir, an English orchestra, an Austrian composer, a German text based on a Hebrew Bible scripture and an English epic poem (Milton's *Paradise Lost)*, an Italian and Swiss audience and, further to the theory that you cannot go anywhere in the world and not find a Newfoundlander, I am in the mix.

There's anticipatory silence in the sparse church. Our concert dress is flimsy and feels colder still looking out at the audience, wisely settled in their outer-wear, their colourful scarves and hats distracting for the moment as we stand patiently during the business of tuning. The oboist – sure but discreet – strikes a tuning fork against his knee, puts it tight to his ear and listens; with the A 440 clear in his head, he sounds the pitch that will tune the orchestra. The strings muck around, so much last minute tinkering; the winds make shorter work of it. Then everything fades, and the audience's bright clothing slips into our peripheral vision, disappearing altogether as we focus.

The orchestra begins eerily, cautiously, as if creeping along an unknown passage. Occasional ominous chords hint at the drama to come, but it is drama reined in, a prolonged, contained drama. In the midst of this representation of chaos, the angel Raphael eases himself in and prepares the listeners quietly, briefly, for the news the choir will bring – the announcement that the Lord has said, "Let there be . . . LIGHT." And in that moment, a grand fortissimo erupts from the choir and the orchestra and the burst of joy inside each and every singer is palpable, as if you are walking at night and with no preparation or explanation, suddenly you are flooded in light. The switch has been activated. God has ended the creation process. The tenor, Uriel, announces cheerily that gloom and chaos are ended; the choir describes hell's spirits forced back into the abyss – they go in despairing, cursing rage, into eternal night. Then, a tender, lyrical celebration of this news: there is a *new* world. *Und eine neue Welt entspringt auf Gottes Wort* – we sing, *A new world springs forth at God's word.*

We stand and listen as the angel, Uriel, relates the story with lines of Biblical text and hints and influences from *Paradise Lost;* when we are not singing, we fall into wonderment as we listen. But we have a role to play; our continuity and commentary are sprinkled through the work. When Adam and Eve sing the world's first duet, pizzicato (plucked) strings tiptoe in triplets as the pair sings – tentatively, gingerly, as if marvelling at their very existence. The choir tenderly punctuates what is happening, as if trying not to intrude on the new pair. Adam and Eve surely cannot hear the mantra of praise gently intoned by the choir – *Blessed be His power, His name be ever magnified* – as this is outside their private moment. We focus – listening, blending, remembering phrasing and dynamics. We're working our bodies – lips, face muscles, and diaphragms. No athlete on the field or in the weight room is working any harder. We are rooted to the task at hand, executing the nuances we have rehearsed and new ones demanded now by the conductor. Yet, at the same time, we have left this worldly chorister's arena of being too hot or too cold, of sore legs and tired arms, of trying not to sneeze, of suppressing a cough – we have left all that behind and wandered onto a higher plane.

In early summer we travelled again, this time to Montpellier to perform at Festival Radio France. We sang a concert version of Verdi's opera *Joan of Arc*. We stood there in our stifling outfits: black tuxedos for men, long-sleeved white blouses and black skirts for women. It was hot, mid-day or early afternoon. We were not far from the Riviera where bathers romped in the waves and lolled in the sun, but we were standing on our risers in an outdoor makeshift theatre in the full power of the scorching sun.

Here we are: I think I am going to die from the heat; the others can hardly bear it and they are Mediterranean. *La chica de Terra Nova* (I was often referred to in the choir as "the girl from Newfoundland") is wilting, expiring. The baton drops and Verdi the dramatist is off. It is hard to believe this man had not experienced

Hollywood. What kind of film scores he would have given us had he worked there. The drama is terrifying and yet, in Verdi fashion, minutes later the musical landscape has changed. From the opening – with its fast, furious strings hammering at us, scaring us, telling us that something terrifying is going to happen – to suddenly, over pizzicato strings, a lone flute singing a simple plaintive phrase. The clarinet follows, then the oboe. We hear a polite dialogue – each one handing off a line to the others – that eases into a tender woodwind trio. This should be enough to bring any listener immediately into the opera, but if not, wait: the great chorus will soon enter. We watch the conductor, we listen to the orchestra, we are ready. One of our first words is a forceful "*Maladetti*!" (Curse you!) And then I am lost, lost in the score, in the rush of sound in the drama of the Maid of Orleans – her story, the unfairness of it all, the heroism, the horror, the defiance, the bravery, her faith. I am part of it! Me, *La Mahjahree,* almost expired from the blazing sun. I am there, part of this huge swelling Mediterranean chorus, this gusty gutsy sound. Oh Glory! I am Italian, Catalan, Spanish, I am Verdi's neighbour, I am a French peasant, I'm a personal friend of Joan of Arc – I'm just plain horrified at the tragedy that's about to unfold. I fear, I shake, quake, tremble, I pray, believe, trust, feel, hope – then sink into despair.

That is how it is with choral singing. The audience sees composure, discipline, training – a uniform, impeccably groomed group. But they don't see what's inside – a collection of individual packages of love and loss, joy and pain, memory and desire – the contents spilling out through the most emotive instrument of all, the voice.

Two hours later, exhausted, parched, nearly dead from heat prostration, I will walk on air, on water, so great is the glory of what we've done. My fellow choristers will trip over themselves to find a snack truck that sells Perrier. I will search in vain for an orange popsicle.

A Chorus Girl at Home: Sing, and Louder Sing

An aged man is but a paltry thing,
A tattered coat upon a stick, unless
Soul clap its hands and sing, and louder sing
For every tatter in its mortal dress . . .
                              W.B. Yeats

I am late for the Christmas gig at the Home. I'm never in a hurry to cross into that country. My feet drag the last hundred yards up the driveway. It's cold but I dawdle, filling my lungs with a supply of clean air. Inside, I gag down the urge to retreat. I hear the choir warming up down the hall and remember why we are here. I throw my coat on a chair at reception, and spread an old newspaper under my dripping boots. Soggy lines stare up at me: ". . . ensuite with master, powder room on main, whirlpool and sauna, view." I head down the hall. The air is hot and oppressive, as if by some olfactory Orwellian trick the walls have been programmed to give off boiled cabbage. I catch up with the choir and file into the auditorium.

We are spared for most of the show, our eyes zoned in on the conductor, our inner eyes squinting to "see" the memorized words and notes. Between each set of songs there is a singalong; now, the conductor at the keyboard, our eyes are free to roam over the singing audience.

Old lips moving, but barely, as snatches of carols come back to them, chests rising and falling in unnaturally short breaths, chopping the long musical phrases we pride ourselves on. Some look as if they might expire in the effort to keep up as the song whizzes by, trying to gather them in. The sleigh is safely home and the passengers content again when I hear a lone rasped "Jingle" come from the front row, but the singer stops herself shyly when she realizes we're all done.

This is not a darkened theatre with unseen patrons. The institutional lighting is unforgiving. I am squeamish and want to turn away. What age does! How it robs and steals as it creeps along our bodies, knocking out power lines: power to walk, to see, to hear. It comes like an electrical storm with its claps of thunder remote at first, distant warnings of the strikes to follow, filling us with fear as we strain to tell if it's approaching or moving off. An attack, one part of the body now in jeopardy, then a reprieve – until the next storm.

I shouldn't avert my eyes, I should look straight out into this community which I will not escape. I think of songwriter Eric Bogle's wounded soldier Willie McBride (in "The Green Fields of France") carried off the ship on his return to Australia: on the pier the crowd is waiting to receive the blind, the lame. Here are those wounded less dramatically, their skills eroded over time, eyes and ears failing slowly, mobility curtailed. Still, a leg gone is a leg gone. My eyes keep coming back to this one woman. She smiles as she sings, and the smile chips away at my memory.

"*Venite adoremus, venite adoremus, venite adoremus Dominum,*" audience and choir together sing. Perhaps it is the Latin that links me to childhood and brings into focus the younger face hidden inside the new old one. The smile has pushed away her wrinkles and muddy make-up and restored a woman I saw every morning of my childhood at the neighbouring church. Then it is as if this one recognition clears my vision and unmasks the others. Familiar features now appear through the crumpled folds and skin. Yes, that is Mr. –, the slightly stooped man who dressed 365 days of the year in a black peaked cap, white silk scarf and navy wool coat. He was a grown-up altar boy, willing to stand in when the boys failed to show. We'd laugh – the sight of him up there in street clothes, chasing after the priest, ringing the bell. These identifications are coming slowly, aided by clues like a gesture or a smile, as if their personalities have outlasted their housing. Those who sit impassive remain mysteries. And now as we sing the chorus of "Angels We Have Heard on High," a man in the front row suddenly perks up and joins us. *Gloooooooooooria in excelsis Deo.* He doesn't look old; some private infirmity has placed him here. It is the change in expression on his face that twigs me: he was a teacher both feared and mocked. These days I read his letters to the editor on social justice, peace, clean water. I will speak to him later to tell him I like his views.

I will? Am I so ageist and egotistical that I think he will be cheered by my approval?

The songs are sentimental. We've been singing "Merry Christmas Past" but the merry seems ironic. And now it starts. The well shored-up self, the one who believed herself prepared for this starts to give way – the lyrics of the song, the faces, the apparatus of suffering are edging in on my resolve to get through this. Don't look. I'm melting. I'm at exactly that moment in life where old age stops being a concept and becomes the place where everyone is – Old Age lumbering towards me, every year more familiar faces in his cart.

It's stuffy here. Open the window, one of the sopranos mouths. More, others indicate with brisk nods and the tall, slim alto, standing near the high window, reaches up again. We will all pass out, the whole choir will pass out. We're on this road together, the road of ancient parents with all the moral, human, even financial issues, the decision making, the transfer of power, of natural order, of who's taking care of whom. We're all on the path, those of us with parents here, and those farther back in the line but on their inevitable way.

"*I remember Christmas past,*" we sing, "*'round the Christmas tree. Funny how those mem'ries last, they come back to me.*" Lines that were too sentimental in rehearsal are now too tough to sing, lines about "*when we all believed.*" Suddenly the song is too much – for it is less about the joy of Christmas than it is about the memory, as if Christmas exists only in anticipation, and in the past. The song snatches even children's happiness and turns it into retrospective pleasure.

> Never can return somehow, mem'ries have to do,
> Younger hearts are learning now Christmas joys we knew;
> All the little children seem to grow so fast,
> But, come December, they'll remember Merry Christmas past.

We are fated, all of us, to be servants of memory.

Christmas: mad traffic, line-ups, excess of food, too much drink. Families mingle, divide, divorce, and throw new faces into the mix. Christmas when hostilities and bitterness are stuffed under the surface long enough to get through the turkey; by the time the pudding is lit, tempers, too, are flaming. Christmas with its evaporating expectations, its residual emptiness. Christmas, when a year's worth of family life is squeezed into short harried days, the family dynamic exercised rigorously.

The December litany intoned by the socialite:
"Twenty coming for Christmas dinner. Twenty!"
"Three parties in one night, I said to Ned…"
"Haven't got time to wipe me arse."
"Busy . . ."
"…..busy………………"
"……………busy……………"
"………………………….busy."

Time chased, pursued. Time parceling himself out in small packages, stingy Time, always shortchanging us and leaving us wanting more, until we arrive at this last stop. Here, where time moves in, settles down, and mocks us. Here, where a sign on the bulletin board last week announced that the choir would come.

"Tomorrow?"
"Not tomorrow, Cissy."
"The next day?"
"No, my love, not this week."
"When?"
"Next week. Thursday, the 19th."

"Not tomorrow, nurse?"

"No Cissy, not tomorrow. The choir comes next week."

Cissy scuffs back to her room in baby steps to begin the familiar eternity between breakfast and lunch.

We are singing, "I heard the bells on Christmas Day, their old familiar carols play" when I am startled by another face, a man my own age who must be here visiting. We used to be related. I stood around a piano and sang with his family for ten Christmases; I remember their traditions better than my own. The Sunday between Christmas and New Year's was reserved for the elderly maiden aunt and bachelor uncle who hosted the biggest feast of the year working for days, like the driven Babette in the film *Babette's Feast*, to produce their secret dishes. And now, instead of holding the alto line, my concentration is slipping – I'm falling somewhere I don't want to go. They are no longer mine. I am the enemy, the one who left. Focus. Think. Add a new harmony. The bread crumbs on the tomato soufflé were the thing.

"Can I get you some more, Marj? You seem to like the 'cazzerole' best this year. I know you didn't like the trifle last year, so I sweetened it – the one with the chocolate on top, that's yours."

Get up from there now; if not, you won't make it through.

Where are we? My neighbouring alto saves me.

Four pieces left, I tell her. Four times three minutes a piece. That gives us twelve minutes more to not look, not think, not feel.

Some have come in mobile beds and specialized chairs. One elderly woman near the front is sitting up in a complicated chair-bed. A younger woman sits beside her, puts her face so close to the old woman's cheeks they must be touching. She looks like she is whispering, but she is singing directly into the old lady's ear, pulling back every few seconds, watching for a response. Forward, singing into the ancient ear, back to observe, forward, back, she is creating a rhythm of her own. There is such love in the gesture, such joy in the younger woman's face when she sees a glimmer in the old eyes. I am singing to them now, they are my private audience until I'm distracted: two rows ahead an old man is trying to clap along with a song but his hands never quite meet.

Across the sea of white hair, with patches of blue and patches of bald, I see a man in his forties sitting with one arm around a frail elderly lady. With his free hand he holds a drink with a straw, offering her small sips. And now a trim, energetic woman steps up in front of the choir and begins to dance. Her rhythm is exact; she is precise in her movements as if she's just arrived from aerobics class. Another woman, less lucky in old age, begins to wave her hands, making large loose gestures like an unruly sign of the cross. Suddenly we realize she is conducting us, mirroring our director.

And in this room of the aged, the bare aged, perhaps there is relief at the release from girdles, buttoned shirts and ties; loose ankle socks welcomed, maybe, where tight stockings used to be. Here, we are beyond the campaigns to persuade us into believing we can purchase mortality with jars of creams and pills. No one torments the elderly, who have less buying power than their teenaged grandchildren. This crowd is left alone.

I swear off every year. I will not go back and do this and yet somehow we know collectively it is the most important thing we do. Later we will tell each other which song beat us down.

"'I'll be Home for Christmas,' that's the one that gets me," says one of the sopranos.

"'White Christmas,'" says another. "We had that Bing Crosby album – "

It's the only bit of music they get, we tell each other.

"Still, next year," one woman brings us up short, "I'm not wearing glasses. I'll come, and I'll sing, but I don't want to see anything." She's still recovering not so much from her father's death here, as from his last years.

I need to share my news, but can't seem to say it: soon, I'll be buying the black marker to label my mother's clothes.

We wrap up: "We Wish You a Merry Christmas." I'm hurrying – aiming for the end of the corridor which will lead me fast into the pure night air. They're in their doorways, willing us to stop, as if they've waited all day for someone to come by, someone with time. At one doorway a well-dressed man in his sixties gives a small kiss to a frail crone. She looks at him, willing him to stay.

He glances at his watch.

"I gotta go, Mother. I'll be in Christmas Eve." He waits for some release.

She reaches for the sleeve of his jacket and tugs him back.

"Don't grow old, Paddy, my son. Don't grow old."

I look at the guy, wondering if he got it, the love she'd just thrown.

Up ahead, four rooms away, a tiny woman with tight blue curls is eyeing me. Even from here I can see her keen expression.

What excuse will be good enough to say no to this woman who, on the day I was born, was as old as I am now? What lie to convince her that five minutes of my time is too much to give, to her for whom a week, a day, an hour are equal in the new math of the aged where numbers don't matter much.

And as I walk the corridors, I am a child again, tagging along with my mother as we made the Christmas rounds, delivering gifts of stationery, chocolates, and smelly soaps. The last stop was here, at the Home. I had the child's horror of hard sights: the legless man who travelled the corridors on a low wooden platform on wheels, the woman whose tongue flapped in and out of her mouth as steady as the wheels of a locomotive, the only strength left to her lodged in involuntary muscles. If we were lucky, Miss T. would come out to the small visitors' room at the reception. If not, we'd have to penetrate the home farther, down those corridors, avoiding eye contact with the lonely, refusing to hear their hellos, shrugging off their attempts to reach out and touch. I was cross-eyed from looking first this way, then that, refusing to admit the images creeping into my peripheral vision. After the old woman's degeneration, worse again: up the elevator to the sick floor.

She was tall, thin, had a full head of dark curly hair, and sat erect in her wheelchair. She was soft-spoken, and had a tender smile never returned by me, the frozen kid counting the seconds to get out of there. Her hands were gnarled, as if they'd been clenched in anger when the wind changed. On the top of the bureau was a black typewriter, and I would paste my eyes on it, focusing on the word Remington.

On the way out, my mother would always make the same remark.

"How she gets those fingers around that keyboard, I don't know. It must take the whole day to type a few lines." But I paid no attention and only years later found in our bookcase a slim orange volume: *Autumn in King's Cove and Other Poems* by Bertille Tobin. I remember one line: *Our brief life here is only night, at close of which will dawn a day with human weakness passed away.*

Now, ahead of me, the exit door comes in sight, promising my life back. A minute later I'm putting on my coat and boots when I hear music from a nearby doorway. I peek in and see an old woman. She's alone in a far corner of the TV room, hunched over a piano, trying to marshal the necessary forces. The crumpled right hand tries to widen itself to make the reach, inching its fingers apart as if each one is pushing Sisyphus' stone. The unruly left hand refuses to be reined in; it hovers over the keyboard like a hunting fish-hawk then drops with a weak crash. Unwanted sharps and flats wander in. Eventually the sounds unscramble and a melody pokes through the cluttered notes. There is a book of carols propped up in front of her, but her eyes are focused far beyond this room. She is playing "by heart," "from memory," and the phrases take on new meaning.

I listen, sly audience of one. The carols carry us on separate secret journeys, wordless travels. In time, I steal away, lifting my booted feet to exit silently.

Conclusion

Out on the water in my small putt-putt jigging the elusive squid, or fishing for cod on the handful of days we are allowed out to catch supper, I am in love with my windswept island. I'm never far from shore with its sheer rocky coastline and thick woods I'm grateful not to be navigating. The osprey that hangs around my house all summer remains circling and diving in the harbour, but I keep my eye on him (or is he observing me?) from the fishing grounds outside. Whales are my companions out here – we've agreed to accept each other. I'm patient with the wind which teases and taunts me, blowing first this way, then that, then – oh yes, it seems so – blowing two ways at once. I look at the sky every few minutes, willing the sun to break through the clouds and brighten the grey. At those moments and later on land when I am struggling to pull carrots from my garden of rocks or when, in the fall of the year, I lie on scrub brush lazily plucking partridgeberries, at those times – and they are many – music is absent from my life. And I don't feel its absence.

Other times, contributing the humble second flute note to majestic introductory chords of a Beethoven symphony or playing in thirds under the first flute in a pretty Schubert line, I've been lost in the beauty of melody and the grandeur of harmony; at those times, place matters not to me. When I sing the music of Haydn in German or Mozart in Latin, I feel giddy with the escalation, the transcendence to a new land. Sometimes I sit alone at the keyboard struggling to learn the piano parts of Schubert lieder – just in case a wandering minstrel strolls by and proposes a walk through those moving, riveting song cycles. I can listen to the opera *A Masked Ball* with the score on my lap, marvelling at Giuseppe Verdi's mastery, or I can shut the book, close my eyes and be there – on a tryst on a lonely path or in a crowded drawing room with lurking murderers. I can be carried into that arena of love, treachery, jealousy, betrayal, forgiveness. And in all this I am relieved from the torments of my own patriotism.

I bask in music that doesn't touch on Newfoundland and I cheerfully inhabit a Newfoundland that is not always tied to music. But there is a point of intersection – one piece, where both feet can stand on the same riser. It is Newfoundland music, but it is also an anthem that can be sung easily in four-part harmony: the "Ode to Newfoundland."

Some quip the "Ode" is "about the weather." True, blinding storm gusts fret the shore and wild waves lash the strand. True, too, that if Newfoundland were emptied of its people, a choir could still legitimately stand and sing a paean to the land battered by winds, waves, and snow. But there are people in the "Ode," and there is a story. The people are implied, the "we" who raise this prayer; the story is the fact that they (we) remain. The "Ode" is an anthem of fidelity.

At Festival 500, the international choral festival which rises every two years in Newfoundland, *every* concert *every* night in *every* venue in St. John's closes with the "Ode to Newfoundland," sung by all choirs on stage and by the audience. Foreign choristers and visitors struggling with English as well as with the unfamiliar music will give it a go. CBC Radio begins its programming in this province every morning with a recording of the "Ode." Rotary Clubs in Newfoundland close their weekly meetings with it, and Newfoundlanders around the piano at a house party will round off a sing-along with the anthem. In short, there are more Odes floating around here than at a conference for Keatsian scholars.

I was on a road trip a few years ago with some young members of the family; they were romping through a child's repertoire – "The Farmer in the Dell" and nursery school songs too new for me to know. Then the five-year-old called out as her next request something unfamiliar that sounded like "Sonrakrow." I said I didn't know it but she insisted I did, repeating the phrase till my ear unscrambled her earnest request. The toddlers wanted to sing "Sun Rays Crown." (The "Ode" opens with the line "When sun rays crown thy pine clad hills . . .") For them it was just another song in the pile of rhymes and ditties they'd learned by rote. I imagine phrases and words such as "when silvern voices tune thy rills," and "thro' spindrift swirl and tempest roar" are an aural muddle now to be sorted out later, as I eventually untangled Hail Marys, Tantum Ergos, Newfoundland songs, my ten times tables and other linguistic jumbles from early childhood. These little girls had no sense yet of the grandeur of music and, as young Canadians, the "Ode" may never become for them what it has been for me. But singing along with them in the car, I was warmed up with the knowledge that, in a place where so much has been lost, this much has been saved. For them, the "Ode" was just another song, cheerfully belted out. For me, it's the happy meeting place of my twin passions: music and Newfoundland.

Acknowledgements

I am grateful to the visible and invisible powers that create and sustain the Banff Centre Writing Studio. This book took shape there under the wise and generous mentoring of Joan Barfoot and Zsuzsi Gartner. Greg Hollingshead, Edna Alford and Mark Jarman also read parts of the manuscript, and I appreciate their good advice.

I acknowledge with gratitude support from The Canada Council for the Arts. I am indebted for various favours to Sister Perpetua Kennedy, PBVM, Wayne Johnston and Joan Clark. For chronic and acute care computer support, I thank my brother John.

Julia Swan swept her keen editorial eye over the manuscript, then swept again. I deeply appreciate Lesley Choyce and Pottersfield Press who lifted a ream of papers from my study and placed a book in readers' hands.

For some acknowledgements, I must reach far back into the past. I thank my brothers John and Bill – my rescue team – who, at the critical junctures, pointed the way. Sister Mary Olivette, PBVM (now Sister Agnes Sesk), led me into sacred choral music, changing my life forever.

Some years ago Patrick O'Flaherty argued me into believing myself a writer. I am grateful to him for this, and so much more.